THE ART OF

outdoorlighting

ROCKPORT

THE ART OF

outdoorlighting

Landscapes with the Beauty of Lighting

RANDALL WHITEHEAD

ROCKPORT PUBLISHERS

First published in the United States of America by
Rockport Publishers, Inc.
33 Commercial Street
Gloucester, Massachusetts 01930-5089
Telephone: (978) 282-9590
Facsimile: (978) 283-2742
www.rockpub.com

ISBN 1-56496-818-9

10 9 8 7 6 5 4 3 2 1

Design: Wren Design, Philadelphia, PA
Cover photo by David Duncan Livingston, lighting design by Jeffrey Werner
Back cover photo (top) by David Duncan Livingston, lighting design by Jeffrey Werner;
                (center) by Yoshihisa Araki and Toshiya Toyoda, lighting design by Kousaku Matsumoto
Photograph of Randall Whitehead by Brad Fowler

Printed in China.

acknowledgments

It takes many talented and generous people to put a book like this together. I am grateful to the designers and architects who shared examples of their terrific work. Please be sure to savor the artistry of the photographers, who have captured the true magic of outdoor lighting on film. Film registers light differently than our eyes do; it is the photographers' incredible technical skills that allow such extraordinary work to visually leap off the page.

I would also like to thank Lou and Annemarie Madison, who have so selflessly given their time and seemingly endless energy to people dealing with AIDS. You are the best!

dedication

I would like to dedicate this book to my mother, Ardy, who, after a valiant fight with cancer, passed away at home on a warm summer night.

She was not just my mom but also my friend and fellow adventurer. My brothers, our families, and I will keep her joyous spirit alive.

I would also like to thank my dad, John, for taking such good care of her for fifty-two wonderful years.

contents

introduction

The purpose of this book is to provide readers with a gallery of extraordinary landscape lighting projects, along with information on how to achieve comparable effects for their own homes or lighting projects.

For many homeowners, exterior lighting consists simply of a pair of lanterns flanking the front door, with a pole lamp at the end of the driveway—unimaginative at best, for the art and science of lighting for exterior spaces has been greatly refined in the past decade or two. Over the last fifteen years, lighting manufacturers have worked with lighting designers and landscape architects to create small, well-shielded luminaires—low-glare, low-wattage multipurpose fixtures that virtually disappear into the overall landscape, gently lighting without overpowering other elements in the outdoor design.

The aim of contemporary lighting for outside spaces is to create a subtle, natural feel. The trend is toward plants, pathways, and sculpture that are *painted with light.* Trees surrounding a home seem to glow in a silvery blue light; walkways and planting beds are illuminated with dappled patterns of light and shadow. This artful effect is referred to as *moon lighting.*

In addition to showing many inspiring examples of lighting design for residential exteriors, this book will illuminate the reader about techniques used by professional lighting designers, along with common lighting mistakes.

It is important to note that a successful overall design may involve a team of professionals who work together to create a cohesive look. Along with a lighting designer, this team can include a landscape designer, a pool contractor, an architect, and an interior designer. But it is the property owners themselves who are the most valuable players on this team; transforming their dreams into an exciting reality becomes the challenge—and delight—of the other players. ◆

firstimpressions

A pair of half-cylinder wall sconces produce a warm corona of light that leads guests into an entry foyer, which features a giant bronze gong. The yellow light matches that of the tall candles on either side.

DESIGN Donald Maxcy, ASID
PHOTO Russell Abraham

Approaching a home at night for the first time offers a wealth of impressions about its residents. Lighting choices are a particularly eloquent aspect of residential design; the well-designed exterior lighting of a home can produce an array of brilliant effects that speak glowingly of those who live there.

There is one basic, overriding fact about outdoor lighting: People are drawn to the brightest source of illumination. Using this knowledge constructively helps lead visitors exactly where you'd like them to go. It is, therefore, logical to place the most light at the front door. Unfortunately, many home owners will use high wattage bulbs in their lanterns. The resulting brightness actually makes it harder to see the surrounding environment, and causes everything else to appear darker. Another unfortunate situation arises when security lighting with motion sensors is installed above a garage door. Created to come on automatically, this type of lighting is harsh, confrontational, and far from inviting. Landscape lighting and security lighting serve two different functions; one should not be negated by the other.

A technique called *light layering* employs a series of task-specific sources of illumination to create a subtle, inviting overall effect for outdoor lighting. Well-hidden luminaires light up plantings and pathways, while decorative fixtures gently lead visitors to the front door. Using this technique, lanterns need only provide a warm glow of illumination to appear as the brightest source of light. Lighting some areas of interest while leaving other areas in shadow, creates a wonderful sense of depth and dimension. For example, a striking Italian-style tile roof needs only a wash of light over a small area to create an evocative sense of that particular architectural detail. In contrast, choosing not to light a perimeter fence can make a property line visually extend into neighboring land-

LEFT As dusk fades to night, this lighting design subtly enhances the architecture of a Tuscan-style home. Shielded floodlights located at the base of the center fountain illuminate the facade, while well lights along the colonnade draw visitors toward the guest house.

LIGHTING DESIGN Randall Whitehead, IALD, ASID Affiliate, and Catherine Ng, IES
ARCHITECT Stan Field
PHOTO Dennis Anderson

scapes. By uplighting a series of palm trees you can provide a living colonnade, leading people to the front door or pool area.

What should one consider when putting together an exterior lighting design? The first step is to conceptualize what needs to be seen at night to create a positive impression of the property. Well-designed landscape lighting gives the viewer all the information they need about the width and depth of the property, how the house rests on the site, the height of mature trees in relation to the residence, etc. Like all good lighting, it will flatter, rather than overpower, the house itself and its surrounding landscaping. ◆

ABOVE A close-up view of one area shows how slim luminaires are integrated with the architectural detailing of the columns. The same style fixture takes on a new feeling when mounted vertically on either side of the arched window.

DESIGN Kousaku Matsumoto, IEI
ARCHITECT Seiji Tanaka
PHOTO Yoshihisa Araki, Toshiya Toyoda

FACING PAGE Two deeply recessed fixtures, tucked into the overhang above the entry, bring out the texture of this front door and potted Japanese maple. Low-key lighting above the pergola casts a striped pattern along the pathway.

DESIGN Alan Lindsley
ARCHITECT Richard Bartlett, AIA
PHOTO Dennis Anderson

RIGHT The entry to the guest house is bathed in silvery, blue-white light. Accent lights, discreetly mounted on the side of the main building, are fitted with custom templates to create the effect of light traveling through branches.

DESIGN Randall Whitehead, IALD, ASID Affiliate, and Catherine Ng, IES
ARCHITECT Stan Field
PHOTO Dennis Anderson

ABOVE Visitors to this residence in Kyoto, Japan, are led through an inner courtyard to the front door. Shielded floodlights located beneath the eaves wash the pathway and planting beds with illumination, allowing decorative wall-mounted fixtures to add sparkle.

LIGHTING DESIGN Kousaku Matsumoto, IEI
ARCHITECT Seiji Tanaka
PHOTO Yoshihisa Araki and Toshiya Toyoda

ABOVE This magnificent home in the Grand Cayman
Islands has an impressive presence that is
heightened through the use of well-placed lighting.
Well lights at the base of the columns help them
stand out from the building's facade and add a
great deal of dimension. The uplit palm trees add
a graceful extension to the colonnade feel.

DESIGN AND ARCHITECTURE Kathleen Buoymaster
PHOTO Dennis Anderson

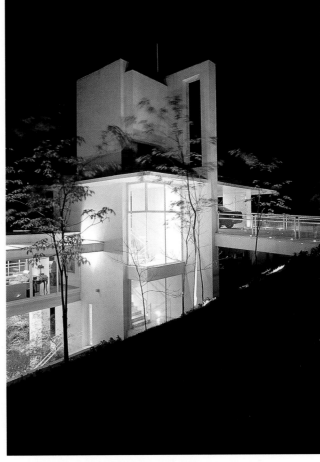

This carport in São Paulo, Brazil, has the feel of an airport runway. Low-profile luminaires flank the driveway. The backlit, oversized house number makes it easy to find this home after dark.

LIGHTING DESIGN AND ARCHITECTURE Guinter Parschalk
PHOTO Andres Otero

Another view of this modern Brazilian home shows how the carport integrates with the main structure. Well lights around the perimeter turn this home into sculpture. The trees are purposely left in silhouette against the white walls.

LIGHTING DESIGN AND ARCHITECTURE Guinter Parschalk
PHOTO Andres Otero

FACING PAGE This commanding residence in the Grand Cayman Islands seems to be guarded by an imposing grove of palms. Well lights shoot illumination up to the canopy of foliage.

DESIGN AND ARCHITECTURE Kathleen Buoymaster
PHOTO Dennis Anderson

Uplighting along the walls of this Swiss-style home casts a dappled pattern of light through the greenery surrounding the property. A pair of low-wattage fixtures to the right and above the front door is all that is needed to define the entrance.

LIGHTING DESIGN Janet Moyer, IALD
PHOTO Kenneth Rice

The high pitch of this wood shake home makes a strong visual statement. Indirect lighting from troffers casts a soft glow of illumination on the warm wood finish. The sense is almost as if one is walking through a large lantern.

LIGHTING DESIGN Janis Huston, IALD, IES
ARCHITECTURE Eric Stine
PHOTO Gary Otte

ABOVE The Japanese-style elements of this home in
Hailey, Idaho, are subtly brought into focus with
discreet, low-voltage linear lighting designed to be
part of the architecture.

LIGHTING DESIGN Randall Whitehead, IALD, ASID Affiliate,
and Catherine Ng, IES
ARCHITECTURE Daryl Charles McMillen Pynn Architects
PHOTO David Alfs

LEFT In winter, the structure of the house is much
more evident. Now the fixtures mounted under the
eaves highlight the crisp, white snow and the
silvery color of the bare branches.

LIGHTING DESIGN Janet Moyer, IALD
PHOTO Kenneth Rice

TOP Water cascades down an illuminated slide into a reflecting pool. The sensual curve of the roof is emphasized with linear low-voltage lighting tucked behind a reveal. Each column of the facade sports an uplit stream of water that splashes into the reflecting pools flanking the front door.

LIGHTING DESIGN AND ARCHITECTURE Lim Chang and Associates
PHOTO Phillip H. Ennis

ABOVE Four low-profile path lights mounted along the coping of the reflecting pool subtly lead guests to the front door. Three rows of adjustable luminaires highlight the stone wall to the right of the door as well as the expansive patio area.

LIGHTING DESIGN AND ARCHITECTURE Lim Chang and Associates
PHOTO Phillip H. Ennis

FACING PAGE A series of pairs of custom up-down lights and recessed downlights leads visually into the entry gallery as well as provides safe passage up the exterior stairway.

LIGHTING DESIGN Linda Ferry, IES, ASID
LANDSCAPE DESIGN Michelle Comeau
ARCHITECTURE Charles Rose
PHOTO Douglas A. Salin

The seeded glass and leaf pattern filigree on this verdigris lantern helps obscure the lightbulb inside, offering instead a soft, diffuse glow.

PHOTOGRAPHY Courtesy of Arroyo Craftsman Lighting, Inc.

Lighting fixtures by BK Lighting are used to accentuate the symmetry and layering of this formal garden, which leads from the residence to the distant pool house; they illuminate a fountain sculpture in the foreground, columns and landscape in the midground, and the pool in the background.

LIGHTING DESIGN Linda Ferry, IES, ASID
PHOTO Douglas A. Salin

ABOVE Distinctive copper fixtures mounted above the windows and flanking the French doors create cones of illumination that add zip to the fine, traditional-style architecture.

LIGHTING DESIGN AND ARCHITECTURE Gary Earl Parsons
PHOTO Muffy Kibbey

LEFT A transparent door with an arched transom functions almost like a lantern at night, as the warm glow of the wall sconces provides a welcoming light through the glass.

LIGHTING DESIGN Randall Whitehead, IALD, ASID Affiliate, and Catherine Ng, IES
ARCHITECTURE Stan Field
PHOTO Dennis Anderson

Miniature low-voltage fixtures mounted in the beam supports of the eyebrow eave provide a warm illumination for the porch. The lanterns, which use 25-watt bulbs, give the impression of providing all the visible light.

LIGHTING DESIGN Richard Perlstein, AIA
ARCHITECTURE Jared Polsky
PHOTO Muffy Kibbey

This very grand entry uses steplights to draw
people toward the front door. Lighting from above
highlights the columns.

LIGHTING DESIGN Dwane Johnson, IESNA
ARCHITECTURE David Ludwig
PHOTO John Sutton

The clean, open lines of this intriguing home invite the eye to travel into the grove of trees in the back yard. Four recessed downlights illuminate the ferns and stone entry.

LIGHTING DESIGN Linda Ferry, IES, ASID
LANDSCAPE DESIGN AND ARCHITECTURE Lee von Hassln
PHOTO Douglas A. Salin

FACING PAGE Visitors literally see right through the entry of this home to the vista beyond. The trompe-l'oeil painting inside frames the outdoor seating area like a still life.

LIGHTING DESIGN Susan Huey
PHOTO Douglas A. Salin

Decorative lanterns integrate well with the
architecture of the house while inconspicuous
accent lights mounted along the roof trusses
illuminate the stone figures.

LIGHTING DESIGN AND LANDSCAPE ARCHITECTURE
Michael Helm
PHOTO Douglas A. Salin

dayandnight

Daylight flattens out landscape design. The sheer volume of natural light gives every-thing an equal value: Neighboring houses, compost piles, and pool equipment are as well lit as the more interesting aspects of outdoor layout.

But when night falls, a new set of rules applies. Now the homeowner or lighting professional has control over illumination, and there is an opportunity to create a whole new feel to the outdoor environment—theatrical, poetic, mysterious. Nighttime provides a chance to design a dazzling, festive atmosphere, to highlight shapely trees, sculpture, and water features in order to create a series of exciting focal points in the garden. In fact, outdoor lighting can be far more dramatic than indoor lighting.

Particularly when the weather is warm, people spend a great deal of time under the stars, entertaining on the porch, patio, and deck and around the pool; these areas take on very different personalities and functions from day to night. Proper lighting can enhance al fresco activity, functionally creating *outdoor rooms* that become extensions of the house. For these spaces, illumination must be bright enough to facilitate safe naviga-tion so that people to move around safely, but placed inconspicuously to provide the necessary light without glare. A well-designed lighting layout utilizes trees and other plants to discreetly hide luminaires; the only fixtures you and your guests should see are those that act as decorative elements in the overall design.

An important design aspect of year-round exterior lighting is the way it works in conjunction with interiors. What is seen through a window during the day completely dis-appears at night, replaced with a dark reflection—the black mirror effect. Clever outdoor lighting can not only eradicate this effect but also can visually expand an interior room. Lighting a planted garden area outside a window, for example, can make that garden feel like part of the room. A well-lit patio off a family room can double the room's perceived dimensions. The rule of thumb is to produce a level of outside illumination that is greater than or equal to the amount of light inside the house.

What is not illuminated can be equally important, from a design perspective. Letting some areas fall into shadow can hide less-than-perfect aspects of the landscape while adding an enhanced sense of depth and dimension. ◆

LEFT At night, this Italianate home becomes a fairytale palace. A stepped series of fountains and reflecting pools invites visitors to the front door.

LIGHTING DESIGN Robert C. Pritikin
PHOTO Dennis Anderson

ABOVE This beautiful desert home uses sculpture and native cacti to draw attention to the front door. The enclosed courtyard offers shelter from the harsh environment and doubles as an outdoor gallery.

RIGHT As day turns to night, well-hidden, low-voltage directional fixtures highlight the glass art in the center of the courtyard. They also light the sculptural cacti that flank the front door; an understated pair of recessed downlights shows visitors its location.

LIGHTING DESIGN AND ARCHITECTURE Gordon Stein
PHOTO Douglas A. Salin

TOP A large parking area dominates the front area of this home, located on the peninsula south of San Francisco.

ABOVE At night, a series of bollards defines the perimeter of the area, allowing the large expanse of driveway to fall into silhouette. The entry to the home stands out invitingly against the surrounding darkness.

LIGHTING DESIGN Randall Whitehead, IALD, ASID Affiliate, and Catherine Ng, IES
ARCHITECTURE Anthony Ngai, AIA
PHOTO Dennis Anderson

ABOVE LEFT During the day, the sun adds dimension to the bronze female figures that appear to be playing along the water's edge.

ABOVE RIGHT In the evening, a series of low-profile accent lights brings the sculptures to life. Selected fixtures are located near the bases of the figures while others are mounted on the pergola above.

LIGHTING DESIGN Jeffrey Werner, ASID
PHOTO David Duncan Livingston

This distinctive light fixture, designed by Kip
Mesirow, becomes a wonderful beacon at night—like
a giant moth perched on the side of the house.

LIGHTING DESIGN Kip Mesirow
ARCHITECTURE Gary Earl Parsons
PHOTO Muffy Kibbey

As evening approaches, this gazebo offers a cozy
sanctuary from the darkness. Uplights in the corner
of the pitched roof enhance the architecture.

LIGHTING DESIGN AND ARCHITECTURE Gary Earl Parsons
PHOTO Muffy Kibbey

These containers of flowers pop into focus with the use of three miniature directional fixtures mounted under the overhang.

LIGHTING DESIGN AND PHOTO David Duncan Livingston

ABOVE During the day, these custom bronze fixtures are affixed to the posts and across the trusses. The entry walkway provides a preview of the courtyard.

LIGHTING DESIGN Linda Ferry, IES, ASID
LANDSCAPE DESIGN David Rudolph
ARCHITECTURE Charles Rose
PHOTO Charles White

FACING PAGE At night, the same bronze fixtures project light down posts while controlling the reflected glare in the 38-foot-long glass-covered trellis.

LIGHTING DESIGN Linda Ferry, IES, ASID
LANDSCAPE DESIGN David Rudolph
ARCHITECTURE Charles Rose
PHOTO Douglas A. Salin

LEFT During the day, sun illuminates the garden and the figurative stone sculpture by David Baughan.

FACING PAGE At night, the same sculpture draws visitors along a pathway to the back of the garden. A tree-mounted, low-voltage directional fixture highlights the piece, casting a soft pattern of shadows through the leaves.

ABOVE This ground-mounted fixture uplights foliage to the right of the sculpture, adding texture to the vignette.

LIGHTING AND LANDSCAPE DESIGN Randall Whitehead, IALD, ASID Affiliate
PHOTO Dennis Anderson

LEFT A contemplative gargoyle resides in the corner of this deck.

BELOW Shadowing and candlelight add a lively touch to the setting. The gargoyle seems to be peering through the darkness.

LIGHTING AND LANDSCAPE DESIGN Randall Whitehead, IALD, ASID Affiliate
PHOTO Dennis Anderson

ABOVE During daylight, this spot in the garden relies on the sun to provide focus and illumination.

LEFT At night, shadow and texture combine to illuminate the same secret garden. Low-voltage fixtures mounted in the trees create the effect. Three candles help set the tone for quiet contemplation.

LIGHTING DESIGN Randall Whitehead, IALD, ASID Affiliate
PHOTO Dennis Anderson

Shadows created by light passing through leafy
eucalyptus branches add mystery and texture to
this small garden. A "doorway to nowhere" provides
a focal point on what was simply a blank wall.

LIGHTING DESIGN Randall Whitehead, IALD, ASID Affiliate
LANDSCAPE DESIGN   Robert Poyas
PHOTO Dennis Anderson

ABOVE At dusk, this hillside retreat presides over the valley below.

RIGHT After dark, artwork enlivens the front door area. The arrow-shaped wall bracket by Pam Morris makes a statement of arrival and warm welcome. Bronze frogs by Richard Clopton are animated with lighting hidden in tree branches.

LIGHTING AND LANDSCAPE DESIGN   Pam Morris
PHOTO Dennis Anderson

ABOVE A stone carved with the word *magic* is spotlit.

LEFT The area is brilliantly, flamboyantly lit at night. Lighting from above the arbor casts an intriguing trellis pattern across the patio floor.

LIGHTING DESIGN Pam Morris and John Pereira
LANDSCAPE AND INTERIOR DESIGN Pam Morris
PHOTO Randall Whitehead

ABOVE LEFT Skylight and windows flood this family room with light during the day.

ABOVE RIGHT At night, indirect lighting fills the interior with light, while fixtures mounted above the window headers illuminate the outside.

LIGHTING DESIGN Becca Foster
ARCHITECTURE Steve Geiszler
PHOTO Sharon Risedorph

ABOVE Daytime gives no hint of how lighting will transform this yard at night.

FACING PAGE In darkness, the shoji acts as a giant projection screen, showing silhouettes of banana trees positioned behind it. A single luminaire dramatically lights up the yucca and adds texture to the stucco wall.

LIGHTING AND LANDSCAPE DESIGN Randall Whitehead, IALD, ASID Affiliate
PHOTO Ben Janken

A 16-foot-tall statue of Zeus seems to point the way along the path; a single ground-mounted directional fixture helps give dimension to the piece. In the foreground, a carved stone seating area offers a place to rest among the shadows.

LIGHTING AND LANDSCAPE DESIGN Jeffrey Werner, ASID
PHOTO David Duncan Livingston

The most exciting new concept in outdoor lighting is known as the *moon lighting effect.* The term comes from the illusion by which an outdoor space is illuminated by the glow of a full moon. Luminaries are mounted among the branches of trees to create dappled patterns of light and shadows along pathways and planter beds, which is very different from more traditional methods of outdoor lighting.

The traditional style of outdoor lighting involves lanterns, pole lights, or pagoda-type fixtures to light porches and walkways. The problem with these fixtures is that they produce blobs of light that do little to illuminate pathways or plants; instead, they draw all the attention to themselves, eclipsing landscaping features and overwhelming architectural details. Choosing to highlight pathways and other features with concealed, low-wattage light sources results in a better-than-natural, moonlit feeling outdoors. The technique allows decorative plantings to act as visual signposts that subtly, safely guide visitors toward the home, allowing them to enjoy landscape features along the way.

Of course, there are practical guidelines to consider when creating a moonlit garden effect. The basic method of achieving moon lighting is to attach low-voltage lighting to trees. Most light fixtures designed for this type of installation are low voltage (12 volt), as opposed to house current (120 volt). Using a transformer, the normal household current is converted to a low-voltage system.

LEFT A series of low-profile well lights beautifully uplights this stand of trees, which is reflected in the black surface of the pond.

LIGHTING DESIGN Janet Moyer, IALD
PHOTO Kenneth Rice

The advantages of low voltage over line voltage are numerous. One, for homeowners, is ease of installation. A low-voltage lighting system does not require the use of burial-rated conduit, as does a line-voltage system. With low-voltage lighting, bulbs and fixtures can be very small, so they disappear among leaves; they also provide a surprisingly good punch of illumination—for example, a 50-watt MR16 lamp (the lighting industry term for lightbulb) can produce 100 watts of illumination for 50 watts of power.

Another important practical consideration is electrical codes. The electrical codes for installing fixtures in trees varies from city to city; it is best to use an electrician experienced in outdoor lighting requirements in your area or, if you are doing the work yourself, to check with the local electrical inspector to see what is required. Some areas allow flexible low-voltage weather-rated cable; others insist on MC, or metal clad, cable, which is a sort of miniconduit the diameter of a pencil.

Mounting fixtures on tree limbs is accomplished with small canopy boxes that are screwed or strapped directly onto branches. The light from these fixtures is then directed through lower branches to project a pattern onto walkways, stairs, and planter beds, and can also highlight sculpture and specimen trees. Tree-mounted luminaires can also be pointed upward to illuminate the canopy of foliage.

The color of light is an important aesthetic concern for nighttime lighting outdoors. Most existing low-voltage fixtures use a halogen light source that, while whiter than standard incandescent light, is far yellower than either daylight or moonlight. Plants tend to look anemic under a yellowish light; under a blue-white, however, they look healthy and green. Many manufacturers now offer filters that eliminate the yellow hue from incandescent sources. They are referred to as *daylight-blue filters, color-correcting filters,* or *ice-blue filters,* and are listed in the accessories section of lighting catalogs. Existing lighting systems can be retrofitted with these filters to create a lush appearance in the garden. ◆

LEFT The primary focus here is the fountain, framed within the more subtly illuminated portico. Fixtures installed below the water line illuminate the female figure from all sides. Two mushroom fixtures light up just enough grass to create rich pools of green to contrast with the white water.

LIGHTING AND LANDSCAPE DESIGN Stephen Krog
PHOTO Phillip H. Ennis

FACING PAGE This secluded pond area benefits greatly from well-hidden light sources tucked among the rocks. They paint the rough surfaces with patterns of subtle illumination. Additional fixtures in the trees cast leafy images onto the ground cover and surface of the water.

LIGHTING DESIGN Linda Ferry, IES, ASID
LANDSCAPE DESIGN Sherma Stewart
ARCHITECTURE David Allen Smith
PHOTO Douglas A. Salin

Hidden lighting creates a rich tapestry of light and shadow. The Japanese maple is illuminated from a pair of well lights below, while luminaires mounted in the tree branches provide dappled illumination for the ground cover. Lily-shaped fixtures provide pathway lighting.

LIGHTING AND LANDSCAPE DESIGN Armand Benedek
PHOTO Phillip H. Ennis

In this estate garden, lighting is employed to create a series of vignettes that guide visitors through the property. Small, directional low-voltage fixtures mounted within the supports of the pergola illuminate the wisteria and create patterns of light along the pathway.

LIGHTING AND LANDSCAPE DESIGN Jeffrey Werner, ASID
PHOTO David Duncan Livingston

Although the driveway is in relative darkness, the
well-illuminated tressels make it easy for guests to
find their way to the house.

LIGHTING DESIGN Janet Moyer, IALD
PHOTO Kenneth Rice

The well-composed lighting of the gazebo and tree makes them the center of attention at night. Notice that no sources of light are visible.

LIGHTING DESIGN Janet Moyer, IALD
PHOTO Kenneth Rice

A combination of uplighting and downlighting accents the feathery quality of these leaves.

LIGHTING DESIGN Janet Moyer, IALD
PHOTO Kenneth Rice

Tree-mounted luminaires outline greenery in light and offer safe illumination for the stairs.

LIGHTING DESIGN Janet Moyer, IALD
PHOTO Kenneth Rice

Small well lights backlight this thicket of bamboo, revealing its intricately woven silhouette.

LIGHTING DESIGN AND PHOTO Linda Ferry, IES, ASID

ABOVE A large-scale lantern sits atop a brick pedestal, drawing visitors toward the front door.

PHOTO Courtesy of Arroyo Craftsman Lighting, Inc.

FACING PAGE A French stone window reproduced by Formations rests among palm fronds and calla lilies, while a stone vessel by Dennis and Leen nests in the undergrowth. This vignette is lit with a miniature low-voltage fixture, tucked under leaves, that highlights the bowl, while tree-mounted luminaires accent the stone piece and provide subtle pathway lighting.

LIGHTING DESIGN Randall Whitehead, IALD, ASID Affiliate
LANDSCAPE DESIGN Jack Shears
INTERIOR DESIGN Timothy Michael Quillen
PHOTO Douglas A. Salin

A fountain, flanked by a pair of graceful cranes,
is the focal point of this yard. Well-hidden accent
lights create the understated effect.

LIGHTING DESIGN AND ARCHITECTURE Wagner Group
PHOTO Paul Bardagjy

ABOVE Guests enjoy a spectacular view of San Francisco Bay from this hot tub perched on a hillside north of Berkeley, California. A pergola offers shade and privacy.

LEFT In the evening, this is the spot to be—relaxed bathers can settle into the luminous, lagoonlike glow of the tub. The uplit pergola creates a canopy of texture, while a ground-mounted exterior luminaire highlights the red-hot poker plants to the left.

LIGHTING, LANDSCAPE, AND INTERIOR DESIGN Pam Morris
PHOTO Dennis Anderson

ABOVE This gate is rather unexciting during the day.

FACING PAGE After dark, however, a verdant and mysteriously lit path leads to a brightly painted totem. Lighting mounted on the house itself provides all necessary illumination.

LIGHTING DESIGN Randall Whitehead, IALD, ASID Affiliate
LANDSCAPE DESIGN Toffer Delaney
PHOTO Dennis Anderson

outdoor lighting | light and shadow

ABOVE This bronze directional fixture by Hadco uplights Australian tree ferns.

LIGHTING DESIGN AND PHOTO Randall Whitehead, IALD, ASID Affiliate
LANDSCAPE DESIGN Toffer Delaney

LEFT This garden is a rich tapestry of color and texture, with the look of a tropical paradise.

FACING PAGE Light and shadow play a big role in how the garden comes alive at night. Low-voltage miniature directional fixtures uplight the tree, ferns, and spiky flax.

LIGHTING DESIGN Randall Whitehead, IALD, ASID Affiliate
LANDSCAPE DESIGN Toffer Delaney
PHOTO Dennis Anderson

ABOVE This outdoor pavilion becomes a seductive eating area at night. Lighting from above highlights the topiary ivy and cross-illuminates the tabletop. The lantern is dimmed to a candlelike glow.

LIGHTING DESIGN Randall Whitehead, IALD, ASID Affiliate
INTERIOR DESIGN Eugene Anthony
PHOTO Christopher Irion

FACING PAGE A female figure by D.I. Constanza hides in the greenery of this tropical garden. Lighting from the right highlights the bronze sculpture and the orchids.

LIGHTING DESIGN Randall Whitehead, IALD, ASID Affiliate
LANDSCAPE DESIGN Jack Shears
INTERIOR DESIGN Timothy Michael Quillen
PHOTO Douglas A. Salin

ABOVE An abstract figurative sculpture seems to ponder the view of the Golden Gate Bridge. Lighting hidden among plantings provides the accent illumination.

LIGHTING DESIGN Dwane Johnson, IESNA
ARCHITECTURE Jared Polsky
PHOTO John Sutton

FACING PAGE A cast-stone maiden holding a bouquet of flowers, produced by the Fenestra Collection, presides over this lush garden. Light from the lower right foreground and from the left enhances the folds of her garment while uplighting the overhanging tropical plants.

LIGHTING DESIGN Randall Whitehead, IALD, ASID Affiliate
LANDSCAPE DESIGN Jack Shears
INTERIOR DESIGN Timothy Michael Quillen
PHOTO Douglas A. Salin

Much of our enjoyment of outdoor spaces occurs while we are inside. Windows become a sort of picture frame, containing the outdoor view as if it were art.

Effective lighting creates the mood of these "living paintings." A grove of gnarly oak trees is stark and striking when illuminated against an ink-black background, while a collection of individually illuminated bonsai trees takes on a tranquil effect, as if in a gallery. Whatever mood is ultimately desired, there is a secret to properly framing the outdoors: adequate outdoor light. Inadequate outdoor light creates the aforementioned black mirror effect, in which we end up looking at our own reflection in a nighttime window. By creating a light level outside that is brighter than or equal to the lighting inside, this effect is eliminated. Do not, however, feel that it is necessary to flood the outside with light—this tends to flatten out the scene.

The first step in planning a lighting design is to decide what you want to see through your windows at night. Compose the picture to maximize the assets of the view; take a good look during the day and pick out the best features from each window. Aim to create a deep, dimensional effect. Perhaps an overhanging branch close to the windows could be uplit, a few grassy planting beds gently lit from tree-mounted luminaires, and, in the distance, an interestingly shaped tree strongly highlighted. Just as in a painting, this gives outdoor garden design a strong sense of foreground, middle ground, and background. Do note that some aspects of a yard should be allowed to fall gracefully into darkness—garbage cans, compost piles, and the back side of the garage are obvious examples.

Of course, not all homes have extensive yard areas. Most city dwellers must satisfy themselves with balconies and postage-stamp gardens; just as with larger outdoor spaces, however, lighting these small but valuable outside areas can visually expand interior space, so that a living or dining room seems to flow out onto the balcony. Cleverly illuminating an overhanging tree expands a nighttime view beyond the boundaries of your own property.

Outside lighting can be turned on with a variety of controls ranging from simple switches to complex multiple-scene systems. These controls can be tied into timers, motion sensors, or photo cells, depending on whether you want the system to come on automatically or not. It is, however, a major error to put outside lights on dimmers; as incandescent lights are dimmed, they become yellower, which is detrimental to the appearance of a garden. Keep light levels at full brightness to maintain a healthy-looking blue-white quality of illumination. ◆

The glass-enclosed walkway appears to float above an outdoor seating area. Recessed fixtures installed in the underside of the walkway provide the illumination. Two low-voltage directional fixtures uplight the tree in the background.

LIGHTING DESIGN Cynthia Bolton Karasik and Thomas Skradski
PHOTO Cynthia Bolton Karasik

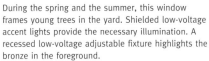

During the spring and the summer, this window frames young trees in the yard. Shielded low-voltage accent lights provide the necessary illumination. A recessed low-voltage adjustable fixture highlights the bronze in the foreground.

LIGHTING DESIGN Janet Moyer, IALD
PHOTO Kenneth Rice

ABOVE As autumn turns to winter the view changes; once leafy trees become a stark testament to the change in season. Eave-mounted lights fare better than ground-mounted luminaires would as the snow begins to pile up.

LIGHTING DESIGN Janet Moyer, IALD
PHOTO Kenneth Rice

FACING PAGE At night, a pair of recessed adjustable fixtures above the table highlight the flowers and cast an intriguing pattern of light on the floor, while the plants outside burst into alluring illumination.

LIGHTING DESIGN Randall Whitehead, IALD, ASID Affiliate
LANDSCAPE DESIGN Toffer Delaney
INTERIOR DESIGN Lawrence Masnada
PHOTO Dennis Anderson

ABOVE This cozy sitting room expands out beyond the window to include a collection of rare orchids. Two low-voltage luminaires mounted above the window line do the lighting trick.

LIGHTING DESIGN Randall Whitehead, IALD, ASID Affiliate
INTERIOR DESIGN Christian Wright
PHOTO Dennis Anderson

LEFT A glass front door opens onto a tranquil water feature illuminated from above. A few selected trees are highlighted in the distance to add depth to the scene.

LIGHTING DESIGN AND PHOTO Cynthia Bolton Karasik
LANDSCAPE DESIGN Chris Hansen-Arner

FACING PAGE This elegant entry gets a boost of visual expansion when the court beyond is illuminated. Fixtures mounted above the door line highlight the two gargoyles on the roof, while a single recessed luminaire lights up statuary and plantings.

INTERIOR AND LIGHTING DESIGN Parish-Hadley Associates
PHOTO Philip H. Ennis

TOP This loop of neon, one of the main focal points at night, takes a back seat to the greenery during the day.

ABOVE Indirect daylight gives the view an even illumination.

LEFT This window frames two striking neon sculptures by Roger Daniells of C.R. Glow. Shielded low-voltage lighting above the windows highlights hanging evergreen branches and the blue Indonesian chair. The palm tree inside provides a visual transition to the outdoors.

LIGHTING AND LANDSCAPE DESIGN Randall Whitehead, IALD, ASID Affiliate
PHOTO Dennis Anderson

ABOVE During the day, the dining room gets its spacious feel from a view of downtown San Francisco, framed by mature poplars. Without outdoor lighting, at night the windows would become black mirrors.

LEFT As night approaches, lighting takes over. It emanates from a neon sculpture and sources above the window line and highlights the surrounding greenery and deck.

LIGHTING AND LANDSCAPE DESIGN Randall Whitehead, IALD, ASID Affiliate
PHOTO Dennis Anderson

A healthy trumpet vine creates a glowing, draperylike effect for this windowscape. Directional lighting mounted above the sight line illuminates outdoor greenery and backlights the orchid sitting on the sill.

LIGHTING AND LANDSCAPE DESIGN Randall Whitehead, IALD, ASID Affiliate
PHOTO Dennis Anderson

ABOVE This tempting vignette shows how, at night, interiors can flow beautifully to the exterior. A good balance of illumination keeps the windows and French doors from becoming dark reflective surfaces; the glass seems to just disappear.

LIGHTING DESIGN Randall Whitehead, IALD, ASID Affiliate
INTERIOR DESIGN Lawrence Masnada
PHOTO Dennis Anderson

RIGHT At night, a pair of recessed adjustable fixtures above the table highlight the flowers and cast an intriguing pattern of light on the floor, while the plants outside burst into alluring illumination.

LIGHTING DESIGN Randall Whitehead, IALD, ASID Affiliate
LANDSCAPE DESIGN Toffer Delaney
INTERIOR DESIGN Lawrence Masnada
PHOTO Dennis Anderson

FACING PAGE A Japanese-style garden adds to the flavor of the interiors. Light fixtures mounted above the window line bring focus to the plantings and waterfall. Uplighting the bamboo inside creates a wonderful shadow pattern.

LIGHTING AND INTERIOR DESIGN Michael Helm
PHOTO Douglas A. Salin

It is extremely difficult to tell which side of this shot is outside and which is inside. The lighting and architecture work in conjunction to create this mirrorlike illusion.

LIGHTING DESIGN AND ARCHITECTURE M.J. Neal
PHOTO Paul Bardagjy

FACING PAGE The upper deck is cross-illuminated using shielded bullet-shaped fixtures. The flowers are illuminated from fixtures mounted on the guest house (not shown).

LIGHTING DESIGN Randall Whitehead, IALD, ASID Affiliate, and Catherine Ng, IES
ARCHITECTURE Mark Thomas
PHOTO Michael Bruk

ABOVE A daytime shot of this dining room shows all of the design elements awaiting night to come alive.

RIGHT The room shows its exciting, entertaining side at night. The wall of glass stays transparent with the help of a series of shielded low-voltage fixtures hidden under the overhang. Candles offer gentle uplighting for diners, while a theatrical projector casts a primal splash of color on the back wall.

LIGHTING, LANDSCAPE, AND INTERIOR DESIGN Pam Morris
PHOTO Dennis Anderson

ABOVE A close-up of the fanciful glass and iron hanging fixture by Pam Morris shows how its fruitlike shape relates to the apple tree beyond the glass.

LIGHTING AND INTERIOR DESIGN Pam Morris
PHOTO Dennis Anderson

ABOVE The forelit geraniums and uplit oaks draw the eye toward the pool area and beyond.

LIGHTING AND INTERIOR DESIGN Michael Hooker
PHOTO Kenneth Rice

FACING PAGE A pyramidal formed glass sculpture by Pam Morris greets visitors as they enter the living room. The tall leaf-shaped torchère, also by Morris, shoots a diamond of light onto the sloped ceiling to enhance the sense of height. Lighting under the eaves illuminates a thick growth of wild iris.

LIGHTING DESIGN Pam Morris and John Pereira
LANDSCAPE AND INTERIOR DESIGN Pam Morris
PHOTO Dennis Anderson

After dark, the foliage outside takes over. The small
bedroom seems to leap through the glass into the
garden beyond. A glowing blown-glass sea creature
by Pam Morris peers toward the outside.

LIGHTING, LANDSCAPE, AND INTERIOR DESIGN Pam Morris
PHOTO Dennis Anderson

Illumination from outside creates striped patterns along the carpet. The blown-glass vessel by Pam Morris sparkles with strings of Italian lights. A stand of trees can be seen through the open doorway; lighting within the branches creates daring slashes of illumination.

LIGHTING DESIGN Pam Morris and Randall Whitehead, IALD, ASID Affiliate
LANDSCAPE AND INTERIOR DESIGN Pam Morris
PHOTO Dennis Anderson

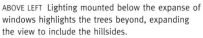
ABOVE LEFT Lighting mounted below the expanse of
windows highlights the trees beyond, expanding
the view to include the hillsides.

LIGHTING DESIGN Linda Ferry, IES, ASID
INTERIOR DESIGN Marilyn Riding
ARCHITECTURE Ravi Varma
PHOTO Douglas A. Salin

ABOVE RIGHT Light creates dimension in this cleanly
designed dining room. Lighting aimed at the trees
outside the window expands the room outward;
uplighting behind the bamboo and the bronze
torso sculpture by David Baughan adds height and
dramatic shadow to the room.

LIGHTING DESIGN Randall Whitehead, IALD, ASID Affiliate
INTERIOR DESIGN Katie Anderson
PHOTO Dennis Anderson

ABOVE Proper lighting balance keeps the glass in this crystal-like space transparent; the pool area and pavilion beyond can be seen with complete clarity.

LIGHTING AND INTERIOR DESIGN Jerry Hettinger
PHOTO Douglas Johnson

LEFT A large window flanked by a pair of Terzanni wall sconces frames the changing room at the end of the pool. Fixtures mounted on the main house illuminate the structure and lawn area.

LIGHTING DESIGN AND ARCHITECTURE John Hood
PHOTO Michael Bruk

waterfeatures

Nothing resonates like the sound of water; whether gently trickling or vigorously bubbling, it clears the mind and soothes the soul. A water feature is therefore a wonderful addition to any outside space. Whether one has an estate-sized yard or just a small deck or balcony, the charm of water prevails. A water feature is particularly useful in city environments, where the sound of water can act as a panacea to honking horns, wailing sirens, and barking dogs.

Fountains, pools, and ponds take on the hue of the light source illuminating them, and while public fountains are regularly turned into shiny blue, green, red, and orange displays for special events or holidays, a more natural color choice is preferable for residential applications. As with most other outdoor lighting, incandescent light is commonly used; amber-hued light, however, turns water yellow. The addition of a light-blue correcting filter will give the water a refreshing, vibrant blue-white quality. A lens with a more intense blue can turn a water feature into a deep azure lagoon.

Placement of illumination is crucial to successful lighting design for water features. One basic: Keep the source of light hidden. For example, the best place to locate illumination for a pool is on the side closest to the house—that is, directed away from the house; this way, when the pool area is viewed from inside, one sees not glare but instead experiences a glowing body of water. Another technique to help hide light sources is the addition of a fountain effect that serves to refill a pool. Locate these spouts above lights, so that the spouting water masks the underlying luminaire; all one sees is refreshing, bubbling, luminescent water.

There is a worldwide residential trend toward installing black-bottomed pools; the dark lining acts as a passive solar collector and helps heat the water—ecologically sound, but, unfortunately, at night the surface of the water becomes a dark mirror. For this type of pool, the best way to add illumination is to uplight surrounding trees and plants, so that they reflect in the pool—an effect that can be quite striking.

Ponds and other still water features should be illuminated differently from pools and fountains. These quieter waters are not usually chlorinated, so algae becomes a consideration; lighting within the body of water highlights the algae, making the water seem murky. A better approach is to treat still ponds as reflecting pools and highlight plantings along the perimeter.

Water does provide some lighting challenges—but when illuminated successfully, it has a magical quality. By considering the above suggestions, a personal oasis is within your reach. ◆

A stately fountain becomes the focal point of this courtyard at night. Water-tight fixtures highlight the fountain from below.

LIGHTING DESIGN Michelle Pheasant
PHOTO Russell Abraham

With the pool lights turned off, the water becomes a mirror, reflecting the inviting glow of the interior lighting. Recessed fixtures located in the overhang help blend the interior and exterior spaces.

LIGHTING DESIGN AND ARCHITECTURE Robert Zinhan
PHOTO Russell Abraham

FACING PAGE Blue filters on pool lights turn the water a deep azure. That color is reflected onto the white facade of this house, creating a crisp contrast between the interior and exterior environments.

LIGHTING DESIGN AND ARCHITECTURE Jerry Hettinger
PHOTO Douglas Johnson

TOP A small, rounded colonnade provides a focal point for this pool, which is built at the crest of a mountain. Ground-mounted low-voltage fixtures uplight the columns and oak trees just enough to keep the pool area from receding into the inky darkness.

LIGHTING DESIGN Randall Whitehead, IALD, ASID Affiliate, and Catherine Ng, IES
ARCHITECTURE Stan Field
PHOTO Dennis Anderson

ABOVE This entire pool area was built around the existing oak tree. A mercury vapor light turns the trunk and branches a deep blue that harmonizes with the color of the water. Shielded wall brackets provide light without glare along the pathway.

LIGHTING DESIGN Jeffrey Werner, ASID
PHOTO David Duncan Livingston

FACING PAGE An artificial creek turns into a waterfall; the pond is lit on the side opposite the fall. Uplights by B-K Lighting are strategically placed among the stones to illuminate this picture.

LIGHTING DESIGN Linda Ferry, IES, ASID
LANDSCAPE DESIGN Michelle Comeau
POOL DESIGN David Cohen
PHOTO Douglas A. Salin

These bronze sculptures are illuminated with
a combination of carefully angled underwater
fixtures and supporting ground-mounted fixtures
focused horizontally. They hide among
surrounding boulders.

LIGHTING DESIGN Linda Ferry, IES, ASID
LANDSCAPE DESIGN Michelle Comeau
POOL DESIGN David Cohen
PHOTO Douglas A. Salin

TOP The lion seems almost amused at having
become a fountain. Three low-voltage fixtures
mounted below the waterline highlight his head
and the papyrus.

LIGHTING DESIGN Janet Moyer, IALD
PHOTO Kenneth Rice

ABOVE The blue-white light in this whirlpool seems
to energize the water. Three tiered wall sconces
provide an Art Deco flavor to the setting.

LIGHTING DESIGN AND ARCHITECTURE Lucky Bennett
PHOTO Douglas Johnson

LEFT This pool area takes on a decidedly regal
tone when the fabric gathered above the water is
backlit. The fabric does an excellent job of muffling
noise when the owners and their guests dine al
fresco around the pool.

LIGHTING DESIGN Barbara Bouyea
ARCHITECTURE Bill Booziotis and Holly Hall
PHOTO Ira Montgomery

ABOVE This magnificent indoor pool was designed to take the cold winters of Idaho in stride. The recess in the ceiling is illuminated with continuous low-voltage linear lighting that uses a long-life xenon source. A series of copper fixtures by Louis Poulsen illuminates the seating areas on either side of the pool.

LIGHTING DESIGN Randall Whitehead, IALD, ASID Affiliate, and Catherine Ng, IES
ARCHITECTURE Daryl Charles McMillen Pynn Architects
PHOTO David Alfs

RIGHT A giant cactus is outlined with miniature string lights, adding a focal point beyond the pool when the surrounding hills disappear into the darkness.

LIGHTING DESIGN AND ARCHITECTURE Lim Chang and Associates
PHOTO Phillip H. Ennis

outdoor **lighting** | **water** features

ABOVE A waterfall is lit by glass fiber optic cables (manufactured by Lucifer Lighting) draped over the top of the water feature. The color can be adjusted by varying the position of a color wheel within the illuminator.

RIGHT A shift in color.

BELOW RIGHT A subtle shift in color.

LIGHTING DESIGN AND ARCHITECTURE Thomas A. Pressly, AIA
PHOTO Kostas Pasvantis

FACING PAGE This bronze monolith glows golden against the dusky sky. Four watertight low-voltage fountain lights project illumination up the length of the piece.

LIGHTING DESIGN, SCULPTURE, AND PHOTO
Archie Held

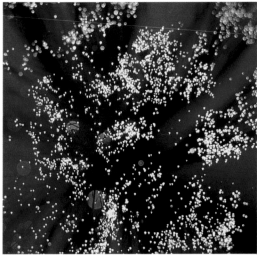

ABOVE Sculpture created from fiber optic components is perfect for poolside art because there is no danger of shock—all that travels through fiber optic bundles is light.

RIGHT A color wheel adds movement and dimension to this piece. The fiber optic components are manufactured by Lucifer Lighting.

LIGHTING DESIGN Jill Giles
PHOTO Kostas Pasvantis

ABOVE Fiber optic light runs along the perimeter
of this pool.

LIGHTING AND POOL DESIGN Rick Ashacher
PHOTO Greg Hursley

ABOVE The luminous feel of this pool area comes from trees lit from within the canopy of foliage and a color filter in the pool that adds a rich blue to the water.

LIGHTING DESIGN AND ARCHITECTURE Wagner Group
PHOTO Paul Bardagjy

FACING PAGE Lighting below the surface of still water illuminates algae, creating a green glow. Ground-mounted directional fixtures highlight trees and boulders.

LIGHTING DESIGN AND ARCHITECTURE Jim Bershof
PHOTO Greg Hursley

outdoor lighting | water features

ABOVE A stepped pattern of gently cascading water adds an alluring background sound to this pool area. Ground-mounted directional fixtures highlight the water and pavilion.

LIGHTING DESIGN Janet Moyer, IALD
INTERIOR DESIGN Bruce Robinson, Allied ASID
PHOTO Douglas A. Salin

FACING PAGE This ornate fountain seems to be wearing a leafy wreath. A pair of low-voltage fixtures cross-illuminates the arbor from below while two fixtures located at the top of the arch accent the gurgling water.

LIGHTING DESIGN Susan Huey
PHOTO Douglas A. Salin

ABOVE A huge pool becomes a deep blue mirror at night.

LIGHTING DESIGN Dwane Johnson, IESNA
ARCHITECTURE David Ludwig
PHOTO John Sutton

RIGHT A subtle row of low-voltage linear light runs along the toe-kick of this rooftop solarium—all that is needed to enjoy the spectacular view beyond the glass enclosure.

LIGHTING DESIGN AND ARCHITECTURE David Gast
PHOTO Douglas A. Salin

FACING PAGE It is a good idea to locate the pool lighting on the house side of the pool so at night the glow of water can be seen without glare.

LIGHTING DESIGN Jerry Hettinger
PHOTO Douglas Johnson

ABOVE A long shot of the space shows how these monoliths have a luminous alluring presence.

RIGHT A glass wall becomes a strong sculptural element in this courtyard when the surface is underlit with pale green neon.

LIGHTING DESIGN AND LANDSCAPE ARCHITECTURE
Toffer Delaney
PHOTO Ian Reeves

This cast-concrete wall gets its glow from two sources: a series of well lights and a collection of candles placed within the insets. The combination is magical.

LIGHTING DESIGN AND LANDSCAPE ARCHITECTURE
Toffer Delaney
PHOTO Ian Reeves

ABOVE A closer look at the edging reveals that a run of fiber optic cable adds the extra punch of illumination along the rim.

LEFT The water seems to have an extra sparkle as it gracefully flows over the edge of the black basin.

LIGHTING DESIGN AND LANDSCAPE ARCHITECTURE
Toffer Delaney
PHOTO Kathryn MacDonald

outdoor**rooms**

A wonderful aspect of warm climates or seasons is the pleasure of living and entertaining outside at night, which opens up a whole new environment that expands the boundaries of a home beyond its walls.

Lighting these spaces does present a challenge, however, largely because there is no ceiling, which is where most interior lighting is installed. Savvy designers employ tall trees, fences, eaves, and gazebos as stand-ins for the overhead surface. When creating "outdoor rooms," lighting can be broken into three categories: accent lighting, task lighting, and ambient lighting.

While paintings and sculpture add dramatic flair to indoor rooms, plantings, water features, and artfully arranged rocks can be likened to art for the outdoors. Accent lighting, which highlights specific outdoor details, can be used to turn a garden area into an artful, fantastic setting that delights the senses.

Accent lighting needs to be located discreetly; there is nothing quite so invasive as a light fixture glaring into your eyes. Shielded luminaires, as opposed to bare-bulb fixtures, help eliminate this problem. Using rocks and ground cover to hide sources of illumination can further reduce glare. The introduction of miniature low-voltage fixtures allows tiny luminaires to provide a big punch of accent illumination. These can be mounted in crevices that would be too small to hide standard fixtures. The result is a dramatically lit exterior whose features seem to glow from within.

LEFT This slate-covered patio is washed with a glow that comes from shielded fixtures installed along the roof line. The long-needle pine is uplit with miniature ground-mounted luminaires while rectangular fixtures mounted in the low wall help guide people along the pathway and steps.

DESIGN Jeffrey Werner, ASID
PHOTO David Duncan Livingston

ABOVE This hanging lantern can be positioned above an outdoor dining table like a chandelier. Translucent glass helps obscure the bulb.

PHOTO Courtesy of Arroyo Craftsman Lighting, Inc.

Task lighting is another aspect of the overall lighting design of outdoor rooms. This is light by which one accomplishes specific tasks, such as cooking at the outdoor grill and retrieving wood from a storage shed. The key to task lighting is to be sure that it does not come on automatically with other sources of illumination; it should be turned on only when needed.

The function of ambient light, as in interior lighting, is to provide a flattering light that provides sufficient illumination to see comfortably. As the name implies, ambient light is soft and diffuse; it gently fills a space without being aimed at a specific feature or task. Ambient light can be illumination bounced off the underside of a cafe-style umbrella, the glow of oversized votive candles, or the soft light of luminous wall-mounted fixtures. Note that it can be challenging to provide adequate light at tables with umbrellas, as the umbrellas may block illumination coming from another source. B-K Lighting has developed a luminaire that solves this problem; it consists of a metal collar that slips onto an umbrella pole. Attached to this collar are two uplights that bounce a soft, flattering indirect light on the underside of the umbrella, creating a lovely, intimate ambient effect.

Layering these three types of lighting creates livable, luminous outdoor spaces that invite lingering. ◆

FACING PAGE Nothing is more inviting than a roaring fire; this fire pit is gas fueled so it is ready for use at a moment's notice—perfect in late September and early October, when the nights have a slight chill. Small adjustable fixtures light up the decks along the edge of the house.

LIGHTING DESIGN Jeffrey Werner, ASID
PHOTO David Duncan Livingston

ABOVE Pool lights reflect light off the glass and wood enclosure; parts of the ceiling slide open to expose the pool area to the moon and stars. A perimeter soffit houses small recessed fixtures that illuminate the slate floor while an accent light, hidden among the rocks, highlights the charming water feature.

LIGHTING DESIGN Jeffrey Werner, ASID
PHOTO David Duncan Livingston

ABOVE A covered patio area becomes an outdoor living room at night, without a single wall or door to block the view of the magnificent twilight sky. Recessed, adjustable low-voltage fixtures offer light for the seating areas, while cylindrical luminaires highlight structural elements.

LIGHTING DESIGN AND ARCHITECTURE David Allen Smith
PHOTO David Duncan Livingston

FACING PAGE A series of brass pylon torchères by Boyd Lighting adds great texture to the stone facade and redwood ceiling of this pool area. A blue filter turns the water a deep indigo color.

LIGHTING DESIGN AND ARCHITECTURE Allen Smithee
PHOTO Russell Abraham

A line of recessed downlights illuminates the
pathway and whirlpool while uplights add an
ambient glow to the wet bar and dining area.

LIGHTING DESIGN Jeffrey Werner, ASID
PHOTO David Duncan Livingston

Small shielded low-voltage fixtures, masked by the wooden pergola, throw illumination on the highly textural plantings surrounding the green house.

LIGHTING DESIGN Janet Moyer, IALD
PHOTO Kenneth Rice

PRECEEDING PAGES Using reflected up-down lights to wash exterior stone walls illuminates this courtyard with a warm, soft glow ideal for entertaining or simply enjoying the evening.

LIGHTING DESIGN Linda Ferry, IES, ASID
LANDSCAPE DESIGN David Rudolph
ARCHITECTURE Charles Rose
PHOTO Charles White

BELOW Miniature directional fixtures, which do a good job of highlighting ivy and wisteria, are tucked among the supports of this wooden balcony enclosure.

LIGHTING DESIGN Janet Moyer, IALD
PHOTO Kenneth Rice

BELOW This rooftop deck offers a wonderful space for outdoor entertaining. Well lights are installed at the bases of columns; they emphasize the curve and texture of the graceful arches, creating a dramatic atmosphere for parties.

DESIGN Craig A. Roeder, IALD
ARCHITECT Hendricks and Wall
PHOTO Robert Ames Cook

ABOVE This patio space needs a facelift to make it a setting worthy of a party.

RIGHT The area is transformed for festive entertaining with eclectic contemporary accessories, including an abundant use of vividly colored silks and velvets for cushions, pillows, slipcovers, and light fixtures.

LIGHTING DESIGN Martina Meyer, Allied ASID, and Lette Birn
INTERIOR DESIGN Martina Meyer
PHOTO Don Gregg

ABOVE Lighting within an umbrella creates an attractive ambience for this outdoor dining area.

LIGHTING DESIGN Janet Moyer, IALD
PHOTO Kenneth Rice

FACING PAGE Thick tropical foliage parts to reveal an intimate dining area for two. Downlighting mounted in the palm illuminates the table. Uplighting adds texture to the lower plantings.

LIGHTING DESIGN Randall Whitehead, IALD, ASID Affiliate
INTERIOR DESIGN Timothy Michael Quillen
LANDSCAPE DESIGN Jack Shears
PHOTO Douglas A. Salin

ABOVE This passageway between two wings of a house takes on a quiet, meditative air at night. Blown-glass pendants lead toward a stained-glass solarium.

FACING PAGE From the other direction, the passageway leads to a patio area with a breathtaking view of the hillsides surrounding the property. Bracket fixtures mounted above the columns provide accent lighting.

LIGHTING DESIGN Dwane Johnson, IESNA
ARCHITECTURE David Ludwig
PHOTO John Sutton

ABOVE A closer look at the patio area reveals that the vaulted ceiling is illuminated with indirect fixtures mounted above each column. A single accent light makes the flower arrangement on the table pop.

LIGHTING DESIGN Dwane Johnson, IESNA
ARCHITECTURE David Ludwig
PHOTO John Sutton

FACING PAGE After a long day the owner can rest on a chaise by J. Art Iron or take a relaxing soak in the hot tub. A wonderful forged-metal wall sconce by Formations is mounted on a support post. Lighting mounted under the upper deck creates intriguing shadows that fall across the deck and plantings.

LIGHTING DESIGN Randall Whitehead, IALD, ASID Affiliate
LANDSCAPE DESIGN Jack Shears
INTERIOR DESIGN Timothy Michael Quillen
PHOTO Douglas A. Salin

ABOVE This area is definitely designed for entertaining. Hurricane candles invite guests up to the table while lighting hidden among the greenery creates a warm, relaxed ambience.

LIGHTING AND INTERIOR DESIGN Suzanne Meyers
PHOTO Douglas Johnson

FACING PAGE Dramatically illuminated columns frame this outdoor eating area. Surface-mounted directional fixtures attached to the sides of the support timbers provide highlighting.

LIGHTING DESIGN Donald Maxcy, ASID
LANDSCAPE DESIGN Harold Broderick
PHOTO Russell Abraham

landscapelightingtechniques

To flatter plantings, sculpture, and outbuildings, landscape lighting must be subtle.
Think artistically when choosing a lighting technique—as in a masterpiece painting, every nuance of color, texture, and shape deserves to be brought out. This consideration allows the fullest appreciation of artful landscaping.

This is rarely accomplished by the all-too-common choice of decorative exterior luminaires. While these fixtures certainly grab attention, they often yield disturbing, too-bright spots that leave all else in silhouette—and may generate only 25 watts of illumination. Select glass that reduces the glare factor. Lanterns typically feature clear or beveled glass that maximizes glare and highlights the unglamorous shape of the lightbulbs inside; frosted, sandblasted, or iridescent stained glass highlights the volume of the lantern instead. (Existing lantern glass may be sandblasted, but remember to have only the inside done, as skin oils create unattractive fingerprints on sandblasted glass exteriors.) It is important to balance a lighting design featuring such lanterns with other techniques.

The following paragraphs summarize the techniques demonstrated in this book. Consider them tools for creating an ideal nighttime landscape. Variety keeps the design interesting; when a single technique is utilized, the result is often a one-dimensional, commercial-looking design.

As the name *uplighting* implies, lights are aimed upward to dramatically illuminate the sculptural quality of trees. The luminaires can be ground mounted or installed below grade. Buried luminaires, known as *well lights,* have limited adjustability and therefore work best for mature trees. Above-ground directional luminaires are more flexible and are

LEFT A dramatic uplit canopy of oak trees rises above this stone entrance—well-concealed. Fixtures from B-K Lighting are used. Custom stainless-steel and bronze wall-mounted fixtures bathe the home's porte cochere and provide ambient light.

LIGHTING DESIGN Linda Ferry, IES, ASID
LANDSCAPE DESIGN Michelle Comeau
ARCHITECTURE Charles Rose
PHOTO Douglas A. Salin

ABOVE A series of recessed fixtures located within the projection of the second floor throws a comfortable level of illumination onto the tile floor of the backyard patio. A pair of shielded directional fixtures mounted on the stucco perimeter wall casts an even fill light onto the facade of the house.

LIGHTING DESIGN AND ARCHITECTURE David Ludwig
PHOTO Mark Trousdale

therefore suitable for lighting younger trees; the luminaires can be adjusted as the trees grow. Use shrubbery to conceal the light source. Below-grade junction boxes bring the luminaires closer to ground level.

Silhouetting is an option for lighting deciduous trees, particularly in winter. The trees are left dark but the wall behind them is illuminated, creating a stark, high-contrast effect. Fluorescent luminaires wash walls in light with low-voltage, long-life lamps. For silhouetting projects located in cold regions, specify a ballast designed for low temperatures.

Downlighting creates a soft umbrella of light over outdoor activity areas, like patios. Gentle, overlapping spreads of illumination cast from luminaires mounted on trellises, eaves, gazebos, and mature trees reduce shadows while producing a comfortable light.

Use *spotlighting* minimally. Statues, sculpture, and specimen plants should be spotlit; they tend to dominate the view as people look outside, like individually lit works in an art gallery.

Path lighting should be approached judiciously. Too often, rows of lights flank a walk or driveway as if it were an airport runway. The effect is especially strong with pagoda-style lights. Consider, instead, an opaque mushroom-type luminaire that projects light downward without drawing attention to itself. This, combined with additional lighting sources, helps create a comfortable exterior environment.

Moon lighting is the most naturalistic technique for lighting an exterior space. It produces a dappled effect, as if the area were lit by a full moon. This is accomplished by mounting luminaires in mature trees, pointing some downward to create patterns and some upward to highlight the foliage.

Less technique than necessity, *security lighting* makes people feel safer—they can see around them and feel less on display than they would otherwise. Further, it provides light such that homeowners can see the cause of a disturbance. The residential exterior need not be lit like the White House, however. Security lighting simply blasts light across a yard, often in response to a motion sensor. It is optimally controlled by panic switches in the master bedroom and in the bedroom of another responsible adult.

Controls divide lighting into switching groups. A typical arrangement puts decorative exterior lights on one switching group, possibly with a timer to ensure they come on automatically. The second switching group includes accent lighting, the third, security lighting.

Resist the temptation to install *dimmers* on exterior light sources; most luminaires use incandescent lamps, which become more amber the dimmer they are set, resulting in plants appearing sickly rather than vibrant. *Colored filters,* too, are best avoided, as they cast plants in an unrealistic color. The sole exception are daylight-blue filters, which remove the amber hue of incandescent lights, producing a flattering blue-white light. This small addition can make a huge difference in the overall look of landscape lighting. Many exterior luminaires suitable for residential installation use fluorescent and H.I.D. light sources. Mercury vapor and metal halide, as well as cooler-colored fluorescent sources, provide wonderfully crisp blue-white light. ◆

ABOVE This striking garden in Japan uses a
minimum of lighting to maximum effect. Carefully
placed uplighting creates areas of illumination that
allow other parts of the garden to fall into
silhouette.

LIGHTING DESIGN Kousaku Matsumoto, IEI
ARCHITECTURE Seiji Tanaka
PHOTO Yoshihisa Araki and Toshiya Toyoda

Hot and cool colors play against each other to
dramatic effect. A high-pressure sodium well light
casts an orange glow on the wall while mercury
vapor lights add fantastic color to a grove of trees.

LIGHTING DESIGN Craig A. Roeder, IALD
PHOTO Robert Ames Cook

outdoor lighting | landscape lighting techniques

ABOVE A series of cylindrical wall brackets provides both uplighting and downlighting for the front porch. Small, shielded low-voltage fixtures mounted under the overhang highlight the surrounding greenery.

LEFT Low-voltage well lights do a great job of illuminating tall redwoods. Small-aperture recessed fixtures fitted into the overhang provide light for low-level plantings.

BELOW The imposing shadow of a Japanese maple looms against a shoji panel; a single ground-mounted directional fixture does the job. Low-voltage fixtures tucked under the eaves illuminate a collection of ornamental grasses.

LIGHTING DESIGN Janet Moyer, IALD
PHOTO Kenneth Rice

ABOVE LEFT In the summer months, lush greenery tumbles into a quiet creek bed. Lighting mounted in tall trees highlights this tranquil setting.

ABOVE RIGHT In winter, the look of this area changes dramatically; however, the fixtures are located to be just as effective in lighting up a snowy scene.

LIGHTING DESIGN Janet Moyer, IALD
PHOTO Kenneth Rice

ABOVE After a long winter, signs of spring appear.
The three trees in the foreground are just
beginning to bud; ground-mounted uplights show
off their delicate intertwining branches.

LEFT In late spring, the trees sport tender new
leaves; the same fixtures light up their new finery.

LIGHTING DESIGN Janet Moyer, IALD
PHOTO Kenneth Rice

outdoor lighting | landscape lighting techniques

FACING PAGE A mighty redwood seems to be reaching for the stars on a clear, moonless night. Low-voltage directional fixtures located near its base project light along the trunk and into the branches.

LIGHTING DESIGN Janet Moyer, IALD
PHOTO Kenneth Rice

ABOVE Signs of spring begin to take form, and the stark, bare trees—each with its own ground-mounted spotlight—prepare for warmer weather.

RIGHT As spring turns to summer, the trees fill out with glorious, vibrant colors. Ground-mounted directional uplights add visual punch to each specimen.

LIGHTING DESIGN Janet Moyer, IALD
PHOTO Kenneth Rice

ABOVE The trunk of this palm is uplit from the base, while its crown is highlighted by fixtures mounted under the eaves. Softly illuminated branches in the foreground provide a frame.

LIGHTING DESIGN Janet Moyer, IALD
PHOTO Kenneth Rice

FACING PAGE At first glance, one does not realize how massive this tree is—until one notices the bench in the foreground. Two line voltage fixtures mounted in a tree off to the left provide the necessary illumination.

LIGHTING DESIGN Janet Moyer, IALD
PHOTO Kenneth Rice

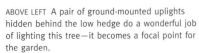

ABOVE LEFT A pair of ground-mounted uplights hidden behind the low hedge do a wonderful job of lighting this tree—it becomes a focal point for the garden.

ABOVE RIGHT As winter approaches, uplights do an equally good job in highlighting intricate branches.

RIGHT Shielded directional luminaires mounted within branches can light up neighboring trees without hot spots.

LIGHTING DESIGN Janet Moyer, IALD
PHOTO Kenneth Rice

ABOVE Trees along the water's edge are softly illuminated from below, their reflection captured in the mirrorlike surface of the lake.

LIGHTING DESIGN Janet Moyer, IALD
PHOTO Kenneth Rice

LEFT Lighting from above and below creates an aura of natural-looking illumination.

LIGHTING DESIGN AND PHOTO Randall Whitehead, IALD, ASID Affiliate

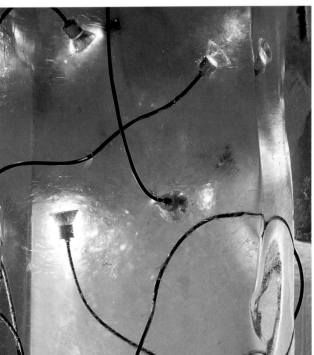

TOP *Fire in Ice* was achieved by freezing sections of glass and plastic fiber optic cable in 400-pound blocks of ice, then piping light into the ice from remote illuminator locations. Each illuminator was outfitted with color wheels to vary the hue of light.

LEFT A close-up.

FACING PAGE This shot shows how the colors change dramatically as the color wheel turns. The fiber optic products are manufactured by Lucifer Lighting.

LIGHTING DESIGN Jill Giles
PHOTO Kostas Pasvantis

Strong horizontal lines do a beautiful job of
concealing lighting fixtures while revealing
architecture. The pair of bollards flanking the path
leading to the front door adds visual sparkle.

LIGHTING DESIGN AND ARCHITECTURE Brian Shore
PHOTO Phillip H. Ennis

Ground-mounted uplights, focused on a weeping
cypress, also paint the rounded walls with shadows.
Two rows of recessed fixtures illuminate wood-
paneled walls leading to the entry.

LIGHTING DESIGN AND ARCHITECTURE Brian Shore
PHOTO Phillip H. Ennis

ABOVE Step lights mounted in the low retaining wall provide safe illumination. Low-voltage accent lights highlight greenery on either side of the front door while, to the left, shadows are cast onto the building's facade.

RIGHT Mushroom-style lights are mounted at each stair landing to provide adequate illumination. The tree to the right is uplit, adding height and visual interest to the landscaping.

LIGHTING DESIGN AND PHOTO
Cynthia Bolton Karasik

Mushroom-style lights are mounted at each stair landing to provide adequate illumination. The tree to the right is uplit, adding height and visual interest to the landscaping.

LIGHTING DESIGN AND PHOTO
Cynthia Bolton Karasik

ABOVE Fiber optic material was permanently fixed in formed concrete steps and risers to create a constellation effect with remote piped light. The fixture components were manufactured by Lucifer Lighting Company.

FACING PAGE The tree canopy and groundscape were illuminated with Lucifer Lighting Scapebeam™ fiber optic downlights and spotlights. Special lenses vary the beam's intensity, color, and spread.

LIGHTING DESIGN Janet Moyer, IALD
LANDSCAPE DESIGN Kevin Shanley
ARCHITECTURE Ted Flato
PHOTO Kostas Pasvantis

Common Mistakes in Outdoor Lighting

Seeing how lighting is done *incorrectly* helps one understand how effective landscape lighting is when designed with skill. The photographs below therefore show poor outdoor lighting choices. Here are mistakes to avoid in outdoor lighting:

- Changing the type of bulb in outdoor luminaires weakens the effect of the original design.

- Using colored lights (except for blue-white filters on incandescent lamps) creates an unflattering, unrealistic look in the garden.

- Using underwater lighting in ponds and other still waters highlights algae and can make the water look dirty.

- Letting plants grow over light fixtures obscures the light source.

- Letting uplights and well lights fill with debris and dead insects mutes or erases the desired effect.

- Installing a bulb too powerful for a light fixture—"overlamping"—results in harsh brightness that makes it difficult to navigate.

- Choosing fixtures that are over or under scale causes visual proportion problems; huge luminaires on small outbuildings and dinky fixtures on big buildings look ridiculous.

- Using security lights as landscape lighting is overkill; the intense light overpowers the surroundings.

- Using pagoda lights is never advisable. These most egotistical of light fixtures draw attention only to themselves and their glare makes it difficult to see anything else.

Of course, not all advice is negative.

Plan

Thinking about lighting during the initial phase of outdoor design is productive. Integrating lighting with overall garden design not only makes the lighting look intentional rather than like an afterthought but also saves energy and money. For example, irrigation trenches can be used to run wiring for the lighting system, and

Mounting exterior fixtures too low makes this building look shorter than it really is.

PHOTO Douglas Johnson

wireways can be put in place before walkways and driveways are laid. It is disheartening indeed to chop up a brand-new driveway in order to run electricity!

The first consideration in conceptualizing lighting design is how outdoor areas will be used. Where will the barbecue be located? Is there an outdoor eating area? How will people move safely between areas? Outdoor rooms need the same consideration as interior rooms.

Choose the Right Light

With so many manufacturers and fixtures available, it is easy to make mistakes. Often the wrong size decorative fixture is selected. It is hard to tell the scale of a fixture from a catalog and even in a showroom. Try to borrow fixtures of various sizes to take home and test; if this is not possible, cut out cardboard templates to help decide on the correct scale.

One common mistake is assuming that mounting hardware is centered on the back of the fixture; in many cases, the connection is at the top or bottom of the back plate. If this is not considered, the result can be fixtures mounted too high or low relative to the front door or windows because of junction boxes mounted at the incorrect height.

Maintenance

A few simple maintenance techniques can keep lighting as vibrant and effective as the day it was installed. Even the most beautifully designed system can be undermined by negligence. The first rule is to replace bulbs when they burn out; be sure that the new bulbs match the old in wattage and beam spread. Consider keeping a supply of replacement lamps in the house.

Ground-mounted luminaires and well lights should be kept free of dirt and leaves. Keep plants from growing over low-level lighting—many fixtures are lost forever in the undergrowth.

Get Help

If the thought of designing a lighting system on your own is daunting, consider using a professional. Lighting as a separate design profession is still new; however, the array of lighting products on the market and of techniques used has created a need for specialists. The expertise of a lighting design professional can save money by targeting needs and preventing bad lighting choices. If you are interested in using a professional—a lighting designer, landscape designer, or architect who specializes in outdoor spaces—ask to see photographs of or visit their other projects, preferably at night. ◆

TOP Consider subtle illumination of the entire facade of a home. Here, ground-mounted lights behind the railing highlight only the lower portion of the house; the architectural detailing along the roof line is totally lost at night.

ABOVE Floodlighting the facade of this house produces a harsh, ghostly effect. In addition, people are confronted with blinding light as they depart.

PHOTO Randall Whitehead

Well lights are recessed in the ground and need to be constantly cleared of leaves and other debris, which can cut out a tremendous amount of light coming from the fixture.

PHOTO Courtesy of Kim Lighting

When laying out the lighting for exterior spaces, keep the view from all the windows in mind. The landscape in this shot is for the living room and dining room windows only. The kitchen in the foreground has no light beyond the windows, which become black mirrors at night.

PHOTO Randall Whitehead

Overlamping—that is, putting high-wattage bulbs in decorative lanterns—is a common lighting mistake. Using a 25-watt bulb instead of a 100-watt bulb actually helps people get where they need to go, without glare.

PHOTO Randall Whitehead

A good technique for lighting sculpture is to illuminate from only one side to enhance the form with shadowing. This female figure is evenly illuminated on all sides, thus losing much of its dimensionality.

PHOTO Ben Janken

Pagoda lights tend to glare, overpowering landscaping. Path lights with shielded tops are a better choice.

PHOTO Courtesy of Kim Lighting

If uplights are to be installed in lawn areas, use low-level plantings or rocks to hide the fixtures from view.

PHOTO Courtesy of Kim Lighting

A mushroom-type fixture is a good choice as a shielded light for pathways and ground cover; however, avoid locating it in a position that draws attention during the day.

PHOTO Courtesy of Kim Lighting

Accent lights mounted halfway up these palm trees
make them appear to be floating.

PHOTO Randall Whitehead

When installing fixtures in trees, be sure to use screws of approved metals. Screws made of ferrous metal such as copper can poison trees.

PHOTO Courtesy of Kim Lighting

Choosing to uplight all the trees in a setting creates an unnatural look.

PHOTO Randall Whitehead

The front yard appears to be only a foot tall when
pagoda lighting is the sole source of illumination.

PHOTO Randall Whitehead

Colored filters should not be used. They make
plants and trees look unreal.

PHOTO Randall Whitehead

Trim around ground-mounted accent lights often; as plantings grow, they create hot spots that draw attention to the location of the light fixtures.

PHOTO Randall Whitehead

There is no illumination for pathways and ground cover if uplighting is the only lighting technique used.

PHOTO Randall Whitehead

The faint amber of incandescent light makes plants
look sickly. Using a blue-white light source, such as
a grow light, keeps them looking vibrant.

PHOTO Courtesy of Kim Lighting

When mounting low-voltage fixtures in gazebos or trees, be sure to check with local electrical codes. Some cities allow flexible plastic-coated wiring to be used, as seen leading into this accent light. Other areas require metal-clad cable or regular conduit.

PHOTO Courtesy of Kim Lighting

Incandescent light makes pool water look yellow. Adding a blue filter keeps the water looking fresh and clean.

PHOTO Randall Whitehead

Using 120-volt lights designed for interior Christmas trees on stairs and along the perimeter of a lawn is hazardous—there is the danger of shock when the ground is wet.

PHOTO Randall Whitehead

Q and A

Are bug lights effective?

Insects are attracted to a blue-white light. Rather than using bug lights, install a blue-white light in the corner of the yard to keep bugs away from the house. Then standard incandescent light can be used around the house itself.

How do I know what size lantern to use by the front door?

Cut templates out of cardboard in the various sizes available and hold them up next to the front door. Please note that the most common mistake here is choosing lanterns that are too small in scale.

For budget do-it-yourselfers, can normal extension cords be used as a power source for garden lighting?

No. Common household extension cords are not rated for outdoor use and could cause severe electric shock to people or pets.

What type of lamp lasts the longest when exposed to the elements?

PAR lamps. They have a thick glass envelope that can be exposed to the elements without cracking.

How does one disguise or hide the power cable from ground- or wall-mounted lamps?

Disguise the wire by running it under eaves, in the ground, through walls, etc. A good electrician will hide wiring well.

How does one mount a fixture on a tree to withstand the force of wind and rain?

To securely mount a fixture to a tree, use a tree mount strap or a miniature junction box designed for landscape lighting.

Is special zoning or permission needed to install outdoor lighting?

This varies by neighborhood; check with your local zoning office and neighborhood association.

**How can one give the impression of more
(or less) space in a landscaped area?**

To make a small space look larger, light the foreground and let the background fall into
shadow. Reverse the process to make a large space look more intimate.

**What are the different types of ground- and
wall-mounted lighting units and their costs?**

Quality of materials creates a wide range in lighting fixture prices. Higher-end fixtures are
often made of cast brass or bronze, while budget fixtures are typically made of a less
expensive material such as steel, plastic, or aluminum.

**What are the major differences to consider
when choosing between ground- and
wall-mounted accent lights?**

Fixtures mounted on the wall may cause glare, particularly when mounted about
eye-level; however, they are good for downlighting plants, shrubs, and large path and
patio areas. Ground-mounted fixtures used for forelighting and silhouetting can be
better hidden within greenery but may not have enough punch to reduce the black mirror
effect. It is therefore useful to employ both types of luminaires.

**How does one mount a fixture on a building
without cracking the brick face or siding?**

To prevent cracking, use a conduit and a surface-mounted junction box. If the wall
is accessible from the inside (for example, in the garage), then wiring can be done
very inconspicuously.

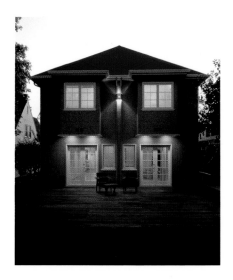

**Are motion-activated outdoor lights cost effective?
How often do the lamps need to be replaced?**

Yes, they are cost effective. Lamp life depends on the type of lamp; PAR lamps generally
last longest. The average rated life of PAR lamps is 2,000 hours, that of household lamps
is 750 hours.

How far away from the house can an outdoor light be placed? For example, to accent the stone at the end of a 50-foot drive, where does the electricity come from? Does the wiring have to go underground?

Electricity can come from the house. The distance it can run depends on the fixture type (line or low-voltage lamps), the number of fixtures, and the location of the transformer. The rule of thumb is that wiring for low-voltage fixtures can be run up to 75 feet away from the transformer without experiencing significant voltage drop (loss of light intensity). The wiring does not have to go underground, technically speaking, but this is far preferable.

Is it possible to have recessed lighting on the outside of a house?

Yes, as long as it is UL-listed for damp or wet locations.

Are some lamp colors better when lighting greenery versus the house itself?

Yes. To light trees, use a fluorescent fixture with a 4100K lamp. Most smaller plants can be lit with MR16 lamps, which are halogen low-voltage lamps. Adding a daylight-blue filter keeps plants looking fresh and green.

How can one keep the costs of electricity down?

Reduce the cost of lighting by using dimmers, timers, sensors, and energy-efficient lamps.

Where does the buzz in dimmed lights come from—the fixture or the bulb?

The bulb filament causes the buzz if the fixture uses line voltage; if the fixture uses low voltage, the transformer, dimmer, or lamp (in that order) may be the cause.

How can one tell how much area a bulb will illuminate?

To assess the ground coverage of a lamp, consider the placement of the fixture—its height and aiming angle—and the beam spread of the lamp used. Test lamps using a plug-in cord and socket.

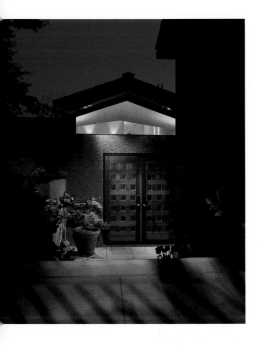

Can one light an outdoor space with candles?
Yes, but a combination of electric and candle light is often optimal. To light an outdoor space with both, hide fixtures so that the light source is not seen—this gives the illusion that the candles are doing all the work.

How can outdoor electric wires be made animal proof?
Pet-proof outdoor wiring by running wire at least 12 inches underground, or through conduit or PVC tubing.

What happens to a light fixture when it rains?
Is there a possibility of electric shock?
As long as the fixture is rated for a wet location, it should be safe when it comes into contact with moisture.

When using an outdoor fluorescent fixture to
light trees and shrubs, what temperature should
the lamp be: 27, 30, 35, 41, or 50K?
41K degrees.

What kind of fixture or lamp is best to use
on water features?
A small landscape fixture capable of producing a blue-white light.

What do the terms moon lighting, backlighting,
and uplighting mean and how is each technique used?
Moon lighting refers to the technique of mounting fixtures high off the ground, generally in trees or on buildings, to create leaf and branch patterns on pathways. Backlighting lights an object from behind, causing it to fall into silhouette. Uplighting lights a plant or tree from its base and washes light up vertical surfaces.

In water features, how does one change
water color with light?
By adding color filters. Blue is recommended for fresh-looking water; other color filters can be added for a more festive look.

How does one determine which areas of
landscape to light?
Take a look at the space during the day to determine what you would like to see at night.

glossary

Absorption: The amount of light taken in by an object instead of being reflected. Dark-colored and matte surfaces have high degrees of absorption.

Accent Lighting: Illumination directed at a particular object in order to draw attention to it.

Ambient Lighting: The soft indirect illumination that fills the volume of a room and creates an inviting glow. Also referred to as fill light.

Amperage: The amount of electrical current that can run through a conductive source.

Ballast: A device that transforms electrical energy used by fluorescent, mercury vapor, high-pressure sodium, and metal halide lamps so that the proper amount of power is provided to the lamp.

Beam Spread: The diameter of the pattern of light produced by a lamp or lamp and luminaire together.

Below Grade: Recessed below ground level.

Black Mirror Lighting: An effect that makes a window look like a dark reflective surface at night. Lighting beyond the window helps lessen the problem.

Bollard: A large, commercial-scale pagoda light.

Bridge System: A two-wire low-voltage cable lighting system.

Cold Cathode: A neon-like electric-discharge light source, often a good option for areas that cannot accommodate fluorescent tubes.

Color Rendering Index (CRI): A scale used to measure how well a lamp illuminates an object's color tones as compared with daylight. Color correction refers to the addition of phosphors to a lamp to create a better CRI.

Daylight-Blue Filter: A light blue glass lens that filters the amber quality out of incandescent light.

Diffusion Filter: A glass lens used to widen and soften light output.

Dimmer: A control that regulates light levels.

Dimming Ballast: A device used for fluorescent lamps to control the light level.

Directional Fixture: Any luminaire with the ability to aim light.

Fiber Optics: An illuminating system composed of a lamp source, fibers, and output optics, used to light an area or object remotely.

Filter: A glass or metal accessory that alters beam patterns.

Fluorescent Lamp: An energy-efficient lamp that produces light by activating the phosphor coating on the inside surface of a glass envelope.

Foot-candle: A measurement of the amount of light hitting a surface.

Framing Projector: A luminaire that can be precisely adjusted to frame an object with light.

Glare, Glare Factor, Glare Bomb: Uncomfortably bright light that becomes the focus of attention rather than the area or object it was meant to illuminate.

Halogen: A gas that recycles tungsten. Halogen lamps burn hotter and brighter than standard incandescent lamps.

High-Intensity Discharge (HID) Lamp: A type of lamp, primarily used in exterior settings, that emits bright, energy-efficient light by electrically activating pressurized gas in a bulb. Mercury vapor, metal halide, and high-pressure sodium lamps are all HID sources.

High-Pressure Sodium Lamp: HID lamp that uses sodium vapor as the light-producing element. It provides a yellow-orange light.

Housing: The above-the-ceiling enclosure for a luminaire's recessed socket and trim.

Incandescent Lamp: The traditional type of lightbulb that produces light through electricity causing a filament to glow.

Junction Box: An enclosure for joining wire behind walls or ceilings.

Kelvin: A measure of color temperature.

Kilowatt: A measure of electrical usage. One thousand watts equals one kilowatt.

Lamp: The lighting industry's term for a light bulb—that is, a glass envelope with a coating, filament, or gas that glows when electricity is applied.

Line Voltage: The 120-volt household current standard in North America. Standard current in Europe is 220 volts.

Louver: A metal accessory used on a luminaire to prevent glare.

Low-Pressure Sodium Lamp: A discharge lamp that uses sodium vapor as the light-producing element. It produces an orange-gray light.

Low-Voltage Lighting: A system that uses a current of less than 50 volts (commonly 12 volts) instead of the standard household current of 120 volts. A transformer converts the electrical power to the appropriate voltage.

Luminaire: The complete light fixture with all parts and lamps (bulbs) necessary for positioning and obtaining power supply.

Mercury Vapor Lamp: An HID lamp in which light emission is radiated mainly from mercury. It can be clear, phosphor coated, or self-ballasted. It produces a bluish light.

Metal Halide Lamp: HID lamp in which light comes from radiation from metal halides. It produces the whitest light of the HID sources.

Mirror Reflector Lamps (i.e., MR11, MR16): Miniature tungsten halogen lamps with a variety of wattages and beam spreads controlled by mirrors positioned in the reflector.

Moon Lighting: A lighting technique in which shielded directional fixtures are mounted in tree branches and directed downward to create a dappled pattern of light and shadow.

Motion Sensor: A device that actives a light fixture or series of fixtures when it detects movement.

Mushroom Light: A shielded pathway fixture that directs light downward without glare.

Neon Light: A glass vacuum tube filled with neon gas and phosphors, frequently formed into signs or letters.

Pagoda Light: A decorative pathway light that has a shape reminiscent of a pagoda. These luminaires have an inherent glare.

Panic Switch: A switch connected to security lighting and usually located in the master bedroom.

PAR Lamps: Lamps (bulbs) with parabolic aluminized reflectors that give exacting beam control ranging from a wide flood to a very narrow spot. PAR lamps can be used outdoors due to their thick glass, which holds up in severe weather conditions.

Photo Sensor: Control device that activates luminaires depending on surrounding light levels.

R Lamp: An incandescent source with a built-in reflecting surface.

Reflectance: The ratio of light reflected from a surface.

RLM Reflector: A luminaire designed to reflect light down, preventing upward transmission.

Silhouetting: A lighting technique in which the background surface behind an object is illuminated while the object itself remains in darkness.

Spread Lens: A glass lens accessory used to diffuse and widen beam patterns.

Stake: A pointed component of a ground-mounted fixture that holds the fixture in place.

Task Lighting: Illumination designed for a work surface so that good light, free of shadows and glare, is present.

Timer: Device that turns a fixture or group of fixtures on and off at specific times.

Transformer: A device that raises or lowers electrical voltage, generally used for low-voltage lights.

Tungsten-Halogen: A tungsten incandescent lamp (bulb) that contains gas and burns hotter and brighter than standard incandescent lamps.

UL: Underwriters Laboratory, an independent testing company for electrical devices.

Uplights: Fixtures that point upward. Those for exterior use are fitted with gasketed lenses to keep water out.

Voltage: A measurement of the pressure of electricity going through a wire.

Voltage Drop: A decrease of electrical pressure in a low-voltage lighting system that occurs as a fixture's distance from the transformer increases, causing a drop in the light output.

Water Feature: A pool area, fountain, waterfall, pond, or other body of water.

Well Lights: Luminaires that are buried in the ground.

White Light: Usually refers to light with a color temperature between 5,000 and 6,250 degrees Kelvin that is composed of the entire visible light spectrum. This light allows all colors in the spectrum on an object's surface to be reflected, providing good color-rendering qualities. Daylight is the most common source of white light.

Xenon: An inert gas used as a component in certain lamps to produce a cooler color temperature than standard incandescence. Xenon results in a longer lamp life than halogen.

directory

Lighting Designers

Barbara Bouyea, IALD, IES
Bouyea and Associates
3811 Turtle Creek Boulevard, Suite 1010
Dallas, TX 75219
Phone: 241-520-6580
Fax: 241-520-6581

Kathleen Buoymaster
6933 La Jolla Boulevard
La Jolla, CA 92037
Phone: 619-456-2850

Linda Ferry, IES, ASID
Architectural Illumination
P.O. Box 2690
Monterey, CA 93942
Phone: 831-649-3711
Fax: 831-375-5897
Email: light@montereybay.com

Becca Foster Lighting Design
27 South Park
San Francisco, CA 94107
Phone: 415-541-0370
Fax: 415-957-5856

Jill Giles
Giles Design, Inc.
429 North St. Mary's Street
San Antonio, TX 78205
Phone: 210-224-8378
Fax: 210-227-5776

Susan Huey
LIT
1747 Scott Street
St. Helena, CA 94574
Phone: 707-963-7813
Fax: 707-963-7814

Janis Huston, IALD, IES
Sand Dollar – A Lighting Design Company
932 Tsawwassen Beach
Tsawwassen, BC V4M2J3
Canada
Phone: 604-943-5641
Fax: 604-943-8783

Dwane Johnson, IESNA
Artistic Lighting Corp.
767 Lincoln Avenue, Suite 8
San Rafael, CA 94901
Phone: 415-456-1656
Fax: 415-457-5483

Cynthia Bolton Karasik
The Lighting Group
3410 Lakeshore Avenue, Suite 207
Oakland, CA 94610
Phone: 510-268-9505
Fax: 510-268-9523
Email: karasik417@AOL.com

Alan Lindsley
Lindsley Architecture and Lighting
221 Main Street, Suite 940
San Francisco, CA 94105
Phone: 415-247-1170
Fax: 415-247-1169
Email: arch-light.com

David Duncan Livingston
1036 Erica Road
Mill Valley, CA 94941
Phone: 415-549-1199
Fax: 415-383-0897

Kousaku Matsumoto, IEI
Kitani Design Associates
City Pole 4-5, 4-Chrome
Awajimachi, Chuo-Ku
Osaka, Japan 541
Phone: 011-81-06-232-1641
Fax: 011-81-06-232-1642

Donald Maxcy, ASID
Maxcy Design
P.O. Box 5507
Carmel, CA 93921
Phone: 408-649-6582
Fax: 408-649-6588

Martina Meyer
Martina Meyer Interior Design
229B Rodriguez Street
Santa Fe, NM 87501
Phone and Fax: 505-988-7425

Pam Morris
Exciting Lighting
14 East Sir Francis Drake Boulevard
Larkspur, CA 94939
Phone: 415-925-0840
Fax: 415-925-1305
Email: pam@pammorris.com

Janet Moyer, IALD
MSH Visual Planners
107 Leversee Road
Brunswick, NY 12182
Phone: 518-235-4756
Fax: 518-235-4756

Catherine Ng, IES, formerly with
Randall Whitehead International
1246 18th Street
San Francisco, CA 94107
Phone: 415-626-1277
Fax: 415-255-8656
Email: rdw@randallwhitehead.com

John Pereira
Electric Light Design
725 Howe Street
San Mateo, CA 94401
Phone: 650-348-3781
Fax: 650-348-7355

Craig A. Roeder and Associates
3829 North Hall Street
Dallas, TX 75219
Phone: 214-528-2300
Fax: 214-521-2300

Thomas Skradski, ASID, MIES
Lumenworks
1121 Ronleigh Way, Suite 1000
Piedmont, CA 94610
Phone and Fax: 510-835-7600

Randall Whitehead, IALD, ASID affiliate
Randall Whitehead International
1246 18th Street
San Francisco, CA 94107
Phone: 415-626-1277
Fax: 415-255-8656
Email: rdw@randallwhitehead.com

Landscape Architects and Designers
Armand Benedek
Armand Benedek and Partners, Ltd.
Hunting Ridge Mall
Bedford Village, NY 10506
Phone: 914-234-9666
Fax: 914-234-6822

Michelle Comeau
Michelle Comeau Landscape Design
P.O. Box 2641
Monterey, CA 93942
Phone: 831-455-1515
Fax: 831-455-1313

Toffer Delaney
T. Delaney, Inc.
156 South Park
San Francisco, CA 94107
Phone: 415-896-2998
Fax: 415-896-2995
Email: dcland@slip.net

Stephen Krog
65 Pondfield Road
Bronxville, NY 10708
Phone: 914-779-2160
Fax: 914-779-1951

Robert Poyas
1206 18th Street
San Francisco, CA 94107
Phone: 415-863-9880
Fax: 415-861-5228

David Rudolph
Rudolph and Associates
53 Miramonte Road
Carmel Valley, CA 93924
Phone: 831-659-3312
Fax: 831-659-0313
E-mail: drcurly@ix.netcom.net

Kevin Shanley
SWA
1245 West 18th Street
Houston, TX 77008
Phone: 713-868-1676
Fax: 713-868-7409

Sherma Stewart
Decorative Arts
P.O. Box 6145
Carmel, CA 93920
Phone: 831-624-8969

Jeffrey Werner, ASID
Werner Design Associates
Redwood City, CA 94062
Phone: 650-367-9033
Fax: 650-367-6587

Interior Designers
Katie Anderson
2745 Mission Street, Suite 16
San Francisco, CA 94114
Phone and Fax: 415-824-8976

Eugene Anthony and Associates
2408 Fillmore Street
San Francisco, CA 94115
Phone: 415-567-9575
Fax: 415-567-9590

Charles Paxton Gremillion
Loyd-Paxton, Inc.
3636 Maple Avenue
Dallas, TX 75219
Phone: 214-521-1521
Fax: 214-522-4438

Jerry Hettinger
J. Hettinger Interiors
200 Hartz Avenue
Danville, CA 94526
Phone: 925-820-9336
Fax: 925-820-9414

Lawrence Masnada
Lawrence Masnada Design
1745 20th Street
San Francisco, CA 94107
Phone: 415-641-8364
Fax: 415-641-0136

Donald Maxcy, ASID
Maxcy Design
824 Lobos
Monterey, CA 93940
Phone: 831-649-6582
Fax: 831-649-6588

Martina Meyer, Allied Member, ASID
405 Ash Street
Mill Valley, CA 94941
Phone: 415-388-3970
Fax: 415-389-8970

Parish-Hadley Associates
41 E. 57th Street
New York, NY 10022
Phone: 212-888-7979
Fax: 212-888-5597

Timothy Michael Quillen
1735 Van Ness Avenue, No. 105
San Francisco, CA 94109
Phone: 415-474-3870
Fax: 415-621-1357

Bruce Robinson, Allied ASID
Bruce Robinson Interior
8010 State Line Road #165
Leawood, KS 66208
Phone: 913-649-0222
Fax: 913-649-7876

Seiji Tanaka
Yoshimura Architects and Associates
14-22, 1-Chrome, Akasaka
Chuo-Ku
Fukuoka, 810 Japan
Phone: 011-092-715-6412
Fax: 011-092-715-6413

Loyd Ray Taylor
Loyd-Paxton, Inc.
3636 Maple Avenue
Dallas, TX 75219
Phone: 214-521-1521
Fax: 214-522-4438

Jeffrey Werner, ASID
Werner Design Associates
Redwood City, CA 94062
Phone: 650-367-9033
Fax: 650-367-6587

Christian Wright
Robert Hering and Associates
151 Vermont Street #7
San Francisco, CA 94103
Phone: 415-863-4144
Fax: 415-863-4152

Architects
Ace Architects
330 2nd Street, Suite 1
Oakland, CA 94607
Phone: 510-452-0775
Fax: 510-452-1175

Richard Bartlett, AIA
Theatre Square, Suite 217
Orinda, CA 94563
Phone: 510-253-2880
Fax: 510-253-2881

Hamlet C. "Lucky" Bennett
78-6697 A Mam La Loa Hwy.
Holua Loa, HI 96725
Phone: 808-322-3375
Fax: 808-322-2664

Jim Bershof
Oz Architecture
1580 Lincoln Street, Suite 200
Denver, CO 80205
Phone: 303-861-5704
Fax: 303-861-9230

Bill Booziotis
Booziotis and Co.
2400A Empire Central Drive
Dallas, TX 75235
Phone: 214-350-5051
Fax: 214-350-5849

George Brook-Kothlow
George Brook-Kothlow and Associates
Lincoln/Ocean Avenue
Carmel, CA 93921
Phone: 831-625-1225

Lim Chang and Associates
35 Hugus Alley, Suite 220
Pasadena, CA 91103
Phone: 626-449-9698
Fax: 626-449-1403

Jeffrey P. Egan, AIA
Daryl Charles McMillen Pynn Architects
P.O. Box 1068
Sun Valley, ID 83353
Phone: 208-622-4656
Fax: 208-726-7108

Stan Field
3631 Evergreen Drive
Palo Alto, CA 94303
Phone: 415-462-9554
Fax: 415-462-9557

Ted Flato
Lake Flato
311 3rd Street, Suite 200
San Antonio, TX 78205
Phone: 210-227-3335
Fax: 210-224-9515

David Gast and Associates
1746 Union Street
San Francisco, CA 94123
Phone: 415-885-2946
Fax: 415-885-2808

Steve Geiszler
Rubel Geiszler McLeod Architects
525 Brannen Street, Suite 308
San Francisco, CA 94107
Phone: 415-243-9440
Fax: 415-243-9490

Fani Danadjieva Hansen, AIA
Hansen Associates
P.O. Box 868
Tiburon, CA 94920
Phone: 415-435-5767
Fax: 415-435-4240

John Hood and Mark Thomas
Hood Thomas Architects
440 Spear Street
San Francisco, CA 94105
Phone: 415-495-2778
Fax: 415-495-3336

David Ludwig
Jared Polsky and Associates
469B Magnolia Avenue
Larkspur, CA 94939
Phone: 415-927-1156
Fax: 415-927-0847

Stuart Narofsky
156 Main
Port Washington, NY 11050
Phone: 516-883-4906
Fax: 516-883-4909

M.J. Neal Architect
1708 Briar Street
Austin, TX 78704
Phone: 512-443-1903
Fax: 512-440-0525
Email: mjneal@flash.net

Anthony Ngai, AIA
A.K. Ngai and Associates
11678 Laurelcrest Drive
Studio City, CA 91604
Phone: 818-763-5567

Guinter Parschalk
RDX-Radix Comercial Ltda
Rua Fernando Falcão, 121
São Paulo, 03180-001 Brazil
Phone: 011-55-11-291-0944
Fax: 011-55-11-608-2257

Jared Polsky
Jared Polsky and Associates
469B Magnolia Avenue
Larkspur, CA 94939
Phone: 415-927-1156
Fax: 415-927-0847

Thomas A. Pressly, AIA
(retired)
6541 North Lakeshore Drive
Shreveport, LA 71107
Phone: 318-929-4055

Charles Rose
25275 Ariba Del Mundo Drive
Carmel, CA 93923
Phone: 831-624-6580
Fax: 831-624-9650

Brian Shore
90 Forest Avenue
Locust Valley, NY 11560
Phone: 516-671-7230
Fax: 516-671-2232

David Allen Smith
David Allen Smith Architects
444 Pearl Street, Suite B2
Monterey, CA 93940
Phone: 831-373-7337
Fax: 831-373-1668

Gordon Stein
Stein and Associates
49858 San Juan Avenue
Palm Desert, CA 92260
Phone: 760-568-3696
Fax: 760-836-1896

Eric Stine
Eric Stine Architecture, Inc.
1-1864 West First Avenue
Vancouver, BC
Canada V6J1G5
Phone: 604-732-4545
Fax 604-736-9493

Seiji Tanaka
Yoshimura Architects and Associates
28 Kamimiyanomae-Cho
Shishigatani, Sakyo-Ku
Kyoto, 606 Japan
Phone: 011-81-075-771-6071
Fax: 011-81-075-761-5937

Ravi Varma
RNM
4611 Teller Avenue #100
Newport Beach, CA 92660
Phone: 714-262-0908

Lee von Hassln
P.O. Box 213
Pebble Beach, CA 93953
Phone: 831-625-6467

Photographers
Russell Abraham Photography
60 Federal Street, Suite 303
San Francisco, CA 94904
Phone: 415-896-6400
Fax: 415-896-6402
Email: rabraham@compuserve.com

David Alfs
P.O. Box 736
Ketchum, ID 83340
Phone: 208-622-7938
Fax: 208-726-4886

Dennis E. Anderson Photography
48 Lucky Drive
Greenbrae, CA 94904
Phone: 415-927-3520
Fax: 415-453-4322

Yoshihisa Araki
Atelier Fukumoto Company
301 Crest Shinsaibashi 4-12-9
Minamisenba, Chuo-Ku
Osaka, 542 Japan
Phone: 011-81-06-245-4680
Fax: 011-81-06-245-4682

Paul Bardagjy Photography
4111C Marathon Boulevard
Austin, TX 78756
Phone: 512-452-9636
Fax: 512-452-6425

Michael Bruk
Photo/Graphics
731 Florida Street
Studio 201
San Francisco, CA 94110
Phone: 415-824-8600
Fax: 415-824-8375

Robert Ames Cook Photography
809 Hickory Highland Drive
Antioch, TN 37013
Phone: 615-591-3270
Fax: 615-591-0937

Phillip H. Ennis Photography
98 Smith Street
Freeport, NY 11520
Phone: 516-379-4273

Don Gregg
Hawthorne Studio
3347 La Avenida de San Marcos
Santa Fe, NM 87505
Phone: 505-471-6128
Fax: 505-471-6128

Greg Hursley
Through the Lens Management
4111C Marathon Boulevard
Austin, TX 78756
Phone: 512-452-9636
Fax: 512-452-6425

Christopher Irion
185 Shipley Street
San Francisco, CA 94107
Phone: 415-896-0752

Ben Janken
48 Agnon Avenue
San Francisco, CA 94112-1102
Phone: 415-206-1645

Douglas Johnson Photography
P.O. Box 984
Danville, CA 94526
Phone: 510-837-4482
Fax: 510-837-7734
Email: rabraham@compuserv.com

Muffy Kibbey Photography
3036 Hillegrass Avenue
Berkeley, CA 94705
Phone: 510-549-1115
Fax: 510-549-1199

David Duncan Livingston Photography
1036 Erica Road
Mill Valley, CA 94941
Phone: 415-549-1199
Fax: 415-383-0897

Kathryn MacDonald
2635 22nd Avenue
San Francisco, CA 94116
Phone 415-681-7506
Fax: 415-681-7389

Ira Montgomery Photography
2406 Converse
Dallas, TX 75207
Phone: 214-638-7288
Fax: 214-638-7980

Paul Morrell
26 Heather Way
Larkspur, CA 94939
Phone: 415-927-8842
Fax: 415-927-0566

Andres Otero
Blick Producoes
Av. Higienopolis, 578/87
Sao Paulo,
01238-000 Brazil
Phone and Fax: 011-55-11-824-0779

Gary Otte
Foto: Otte Photo
21-1551 Johnson Street
Granville Island, Vancouver, BC
Canada U6H3R9
Phone: 604-681-8421

Kostas Pasvantis
Bierweg 28, 1261 BL
Blaricum, Netherlands
Phone: 011-31-35-538-7673
Fax: 011-31-35-538-9356

Ian Reeves
2140 Bush Street, Suite 3
San Francisco, CA 91445
Phone: 415-775-0300
Fax: 415-447-2711

Kenneth Rice Photography
456 61st Street
Oakland, CA 94103
Phone: 510-652-1752
Fax: 510-658-4355

Sharon Risedorph Photography
761 Clementina Street
San Francisco, CA 94106
Phone: 415-431-5851

Douglas A. Salin Photography
647 Joost Avenue
San Francisco, CA 94127
Phone: 415-584-3322
Pager: 415-227-6600

John Sutton Photography
8 Main Street
Point San Quentin, CA 94964
Phone: 415-258-8100
Fax: 415-258-1167

Toshiya Toyoda
Toyoda Photo Studio
1-3611 Sakuraoka, Shime-cho
Kasuyagun, Fukuoka 811-22
Japan
Phone: 011-092-935-7987

Mark Trousdale
2849AA Fillmore Street
San Francisco, CA 94123
Phone: 415-931-0564

Charles White, Photographer
154 North Mansfield Avenue
Los Angeles, CA 90036
Phone: 323-937-3117
Fax: 323-937-1808

Randall Whitehead, IALD, ASID Affiliate
Randall Whitehead International
1246 18th Street
San Francisco, CA 94107
Phone: 415-626-1210
Fax: 415-626-1821
Email: rdw@randallwhitehead.com

Pool Designers
David Cohen
Custom Water Effects
P.O. Box 1842
Soquel, CA 95073
Phone: 408-476-7794
Fax: 303-861-9230

Lighting Fixture Designers and Manufacturers
Arroyo Craftsman Lighting, Inc.
4509 Little John Street
Baldwin Park, CA 91706
Phone: 626-960-9411
Fax: 626-960-9521

B-K Lighting
7595 North Delmar Avenue
Fresno, CA 93711
Phone: 209-438-5800
Fax: 209-438-5900

Boyd Lighting
944 Folsom Street
San Francisco, CA 94107-1007
Phone: 415-778-4300
Fax: 415-778-4319
Email: info@boydlighting.com

Roger Daniells
C.R. Glow
10 West Norwich
Stockton, CA 95207
Pager: 209-982-7801
Fax: 209-952-9715
Email: crglow@jps.net

Hadco Architectural Outdoor Lighting
P.O. Box 128
100 Craftway
Littlestown, PA 17340
Phone: 717-359-7131
Fax: 717-359-9289

Kim Lighting
16555 East Gale Avenue
P.O. Box 1275
City of Industry, CA 91749
Phone: 818-968-5666
Fax: 818-369-2695

Loran Nightscaping, Inc.
1705 East Colton Avenue
Redlands, CA 92374
Phone: 909-794-2121
Fax: 909-794-7292

Gilbert Lang Mathews
Lucifer Lighting Company
414 Live Oak Street
San Antonio, TX 78202
Phone: 210-227-7329
Fax: 210-227-4967

Lumiere Design and Manufacturing, Inc.
2382 Townsgate Road
Westlake Village, CA 91361
Phone: 805-496-2003
Fax: 805-496-2303
Website: www.lumieredesign.com

Pam Morris
Exciting Lighting
14 East Sir Francis Drake Boulevard
Larkspur, CA 94939
Phone: 415-925-0840
Fax: 415-925-1305
Email: pam@pammorris.com